MW01200222

Aztec

A Captivating Guide to Aztec History and the Triple Alliance of Tenochtitlan, Tetzcoco, and Tlacopan

Contents

Free Bonus from Captivating History (Available for a Limited time)

Hi History Lovers!

Now you have a chance to join our exclusive history list so you can get your first history ebook for free as well as discounts and a potential to get more history books for free! Simply visit the link below to join.

Captivatinghistory.com/ebook

Also, make sure to follow us on:

Twitter: @Captivhistory

Facebook: Captivating History:
@captivatinghistory

Introduction

Nothing remains of the ancient Mesoamerican civilization who called themselves the Mexica, better known to us as the Aztecs. Nothing except for their remarkable story.

In this book, we discuss their enigmatic origins and how the Aztecs rose from nomadic tribes to the dominant power in Mesoamerica at an astounding speed. You'll wander the streets of their great capital city of Tenochtitlán, known as "the Venice of the New World" among the Spanish Conquistadors, who spread the term all over Europe. You'll discover the full extent of the city's splendour, visiting its many market stalls, smelling fresh chocolate and vanilla pods. You'll indulge in a taste of ripe, hand-picked avocados and freshly baked corn tortillas, as you decipher Náhuatl, the language spoken by the 50,000 merchants who visited Tenochtitlán every day.

You'll probably wonder how this great city, built in the middle of a lake and isolated by two of Mexico's highest mountains, Iztaccihuatl and Popocatepetl, could ever be defeated. From the arrival of the first Spaniards in 1519 to the eventual fall of the Aztec empire, we'll talk you through the major battles that eventually led to its fall. We'll uncover lies and deceptions in the alliance with their neighbouring cities of Tetzcoco and Tlacopan. We'll also look at Aztec legacy on the world today: how Tenochtitlán became the basis for the capital of the New World and evolved into today's Mexico City.

Remember the most interesting stories are peppered with fascinating contrasts and paradoxes. Perhaps this is what makes the

Aztecs so interesting. They emulated and idolized the Toltec civilization in everything they did, although there's no archeological evidence to support that the great Toltec civilization even existed. Each year, the Aztecs performed a substantial number of brutal human sacrifices, yet they were also completely devoted to intellectual pursuits, such as mathematics, public speaking, and the arts.

Masters of their own fate, the Aztecs re-wrote their story of origin, burning their history books. This has enmeshed much of their history with mythology and made it difficult to separate myth from fact. Further complications were caused by the Spanish conquistadors and their successors, who wanted to portray themselves in a good light or justify their conquest when writing their accounts of the Aztecs.

Chapter 1 – The Origins of Aztecs: A Tribe Destined for Greatness

On the Mexican flag backdrop of a vertical tricolour of green, white, and red, a fierce eagle sits on top of a cactus plant, wrestling with a snake that it's snatched in its mouth. This is the symbol of the Aztec city of Tenochtitlán and tells the story of how a humble tribe from the North, who called themselves the Mexica, rose to astonishing wealth and power just a few hundred years after finding their 'promised land,' known today as Mexico City.

Let's look at the origins of the Mexica civilization, better known to us by the name of the Aztecs.

Rewriting Aztec history

The story of their origin is obscured by legend. The Aztecs arrived and settled in the Valley of Mexico around the year 1250 AD, and they most likely came from the North. Thanks to a tyrannical move by one of their kings, Itzcoatl, who ruled the Aztec empire from 1427 to 1440, all the books that told the story of Aztec history up to that point were burned.

The son of a slave woman and a nobleman, Itzcoatl quickly rose to power, thanks to his military achievements. He was set for greatness, and, perhaps to erase his heritage of being born to a slave woman, he made earnest efforts to rewrite the history of the Aztecs to create a more palatable version of their origins.

Another book-burning incident took place much later, destroying more crucial information about the Aztecs. It was done to heavily censor the Florentine Codex, a 12-volume work by the Franciscan monk Bernardino de Sahagún. He spent years interviewing the local tribes, learning about the ancient Aztec language of Náhuatl and their many rites and customs. When he returned to Europe in 1585, the Spanish authorities confiscated much of his original material, destroying this valuable resource. The later versions of the Florentine Codex that did get published were most likely heavily censored, erasing many captivating details that would have shed light on the Aztecs and other ancient Mesoamerican cultures.

Because of these unfortunate instances, what we know of the origins of the Aztec civilization are draped in myth, and subject to much speculation by archaeologists and historians.

Aztlán - the cradle of Aztec civilization

Aztlán is a bit like Atlantis, a legendary ancient land that disappeared and has puzzled researchers for years. Even the Aztecs were fascinated with finding the mystical land of Aztlán. Similar to King Arthur's mission to find the Holy Grail, the Aztec ruler Montezuma I gathered his fiercest warriors and most knowledgeable scholars in the 1450s and sent them on a mission to find Aztlán. Apparently, they succeeded, although the maps they drew have not survived, so their success remains debatable. It was said to be located somewhere to the north of Tenochtitlán, and, like the Aztecs' great city, Aztlán too was in the middle of a lake.

While it could be nothing more than Aztec propaganda to depict an idealized version of their origins and to support their claim of rulership, the myth of Aztlán is fascinating. It was incredibly important to the Aztecs too - the term Aztec means "the people of Aztlán." Although the Aztecs called themselves the Mexica, they did regard themselves as the direct descendants of the tribe that used to live in Aztlán.

The myth of Aztlán

When the Spanish arrived in Mexico in the 16th century, they became fascinated by the Aztec culture. They made several attempts to document their origin story, and parts of it were recorded by Diego Duran, a Dominican friar who arrived in the New World in 1540 when he was five years old. A document called *Los Anales de Tlatelolco* (The Annals of Tlatelolco), now held at the National Library of France in Paris, also reveals much about the lost land of Aztlán.

These accounts reveal the fascinating story of Aztlán and the origins of the Aztec civilization. Translated, the word "Aztlán" stands for "the place of white birds" or "the place of herons." According to legend, the Aztec emerged from the hollow earth through a system of caves, along with six other tribes (Acolhua, Chalca, Tepaneca, Tlahuica, Tlaxcalan, and Xochimilca).

A depiction of Chicomoztoc — the place of the seven caves. Source: https://en.wikipedia.org/wiki/Aztl%C3%A1n

The seven tribes wandered the Earth together, sometime between the years of 1100 and 1300. Then the other tribes decided to migrate south while the Aztecs remained in the north. They eventually found their "paradise," called Aztlán. It was a large island in the middle of lake Metztliapan ("the lake of the Moon").

The science of linguistics can help trace the true origins of Aztlán. The Aztec language of Náhuatl comes from the Uto-Aztecan language tree. Robert Bitto explores this further in his podcast *Journey to Aztlán, the Mythical Homeland of the Aztecs*. He explains that several tribes who lived to the north of Mexico spoke a language that belonged to the same language tree. Along with some indigenous tribes from northern Mexico, these include the Hopi, the Pima, and the Utes of Utah, USA. The linguistic connection stretches as far as Idaho and Montana, supporting the claim the Aztecs did come from the north. Scholars agree the most likely location for Aztlán is in the northern or central parts of Mexico.

Considering that Aztlán was as good as paradise, why did the Aztecs decide to leave?

The fall of Aztlán

Some accounts state the Aztecs fled because they were encroached upon by a tyrannical ruling elite that wanted them expelled or enslaved. Once they began to flee, they were pushed further and further south by the Chichimecas, a warlike marauding tribe.

Other accounts state there was a natural disaster of such a magnitude it drove the Aztecs out of the area and forced them to migrate south. Climatic studies conducted in the region support this claim, stating that between the years of 1100 and 1300 a mass migration occurred to the south-west of the modern-day United States. This was most likely because of a lengthy period of drought. The Aztecs left the area around 1200 AD, so this theory is plausible.

After leaving Aztlán, the Aztecs became a nomadic tribe, wandering the plains of northern Mexico, and making their way south for two hundred years. They endured many hardships along the way before they eventually settled on the tiny island in the middle of Lake Texcoco in the Valley of Mexico, where they founded their great city of Tenochtitlán. According to legend, the Aztecs were guided and seen through their hardships by a deity called Huitzilopochtli, the Aztec god of war, the sun, and human sacrifice. He was later the patron god of the city of Tenochtitlán.

But it wasn't a straight journey, and by no means easy either. The Aztecs made several stops along the way, even settling temporarily in some of these areas. At times, some of the Aztecs wanted to remain and began opposing the priests who urged them to keep moving. Battles broke out amidst their own people, as they wandered the land for nearly two hundred years, from hardship to hardship. Until they finally arrived in the Valley of Mexico. But the welcome they received wasn't quite what they'd expected.

Chapter 2 – The Unwelcome Arrival in Mexico Valley

After two hundred years of exile, the Aztec was on a quest to find a new homeland. They had finally reached the Valley of Mexico, where their priests had guided them and instructed them to settle. However, they were not welcomed by the locals, who were wary of foreigners. Their journey had been hard, but life was not about to get any easier for the Aztecs.

They arrived in the Valley of Mexico around the year 1300 AD. The valley was bustling with various tribes and civilizations, most of them rivals. Professor Edwin Barnhart explains what happened to the Aztecs after they arrived in Mexico Valley and before they founded their great capital of Tenochtitlán in chapter 33 of his lecture series *Maya to Aztec: Ancient Mesoamerica Revealed*. According to him, the Aztecs were "outnumbered, outranked, and outclassed," a stark contrast to the bustling civilization the Spaniards found just over 200 years later.

Two of these rival tribes were larger than the rest - the Tepanecs and the Culhuacan. The Tepanecs allowed the Aztecs to settle, granting them Chapultepec or "the grasshopper hill." It was situated on the west shore of Lake Texcoco, now the central park of Mexico City. Their subway system also features icons relating back to this period - one of the stops is depicted as a hill with an ant on it, symbolizing the grasshopper hill.

The Tepanecs were a dominant force in the area, taking over after the Toltec empire fell around 1200 AD. Many cultures around the time, including the Aztecs, went to great lengths to claim themselves as descendants of the ancient Toltec civilization and to emulate their achievements. However, the Toltec civilization may have never existed at all.

Settling in Chapultepec

It wasn't long before the Teponecs grew annoyed with the Aztecs. Less than a year later, they kicked them out. At this point in history, the Aztecs acted like savages. They didn't pay their tributes to the Tepanecs, and were considered uncultured savages.

The Aztecs fled Chapultepec and travelled south. They reached the area controlled by the Culhuacan, who granted the Aztecs a barren land known as Tizapan. It was infertile and impossible to farm. The Aztec diet consisted mainly of lizards and rodents.

But their god Huitzilipochtli was never far from them, at least according to the Aztec priests who provided guidance. They said the Aztecs should take up deeds that honoured the war god and do the 'dirty work' that no one else wanted to do. This helped the Aztecs to develop a sophisticated warrior culture.

This tactic paid off. Twenty years later, the Aztecs had intermarried with the people of Culhuacan and their children were immersed in their culture. After more than two hundred years of unrest, things were finally looking up for the Aztecs, until one fatal day that changed everything.

Sacrifice gone wrong

It's important to understand the meaning of human sacrifice for the Aztecs. They believed sacrifice was a welcome offering to their gods, and many people gladly engaged in acts of self-mutilation. Sacrifice was often a way to get closer to the gods, so when Achicometl, the ruler of Culhuacan, offered his daughter to the Aztecs for marriage in 1323, they thought it would be a better idea to sacrifice her to their gods. In turn, this would make the king's daughter into a goddess.

Except Achicometl did not see it that way. One day, he saw one of the Aztec priests wearing the flayed skin of his daughter during a festival dinner. Far from thanking the Aztecs for their attempt to make his daughter into a deity, he was so horrified he cast them out. Somewhat confused, the Aztecs were forced to wander the Valley of Mexico once more.

The vision of their new home

One day, as they wandered around Lake Texcoco to find their new home, their high priest had a vision. "Our promised land will be marked by an eagle, sat on a cactus, holding a snake in its mouth," he announced, coming out of his trance. The Aztecs didn't have their own land yet, but at least they had a sign of what they were looking for.

The symbol of an eagle sat on a cactus with a snake in its mouth on the flag of Mexico. Source: https://www.tripsavvy.com/the-mexican-flag-1588860

Hopeful, they settled with the Teponecs once again. Having learned their lesson, the Aztecs paid tribute to the Teponecs and fought for them. They added more problems in the valley where several tribes and cultures were already fighting each other. They fought against Culhuacan while searching for the sacred sign that would mark their new home.

Two years later, their priest finally saw the sign. Huitzilipochtli certainly wasn't giving them an easy time - their promised land was in the middle of a lake on a tiny island. Shallow, marshy land made up the island, but the Aztecs followed their god and settled there. In 1325, the Aztecs began to build Tenochtitlán on the island. Little did they know that a hundred years later the Aztecs would dominate the entire region, and this tiny island would become one of the greatest cities that Mesoamerica had ever seen.

Building a city on a lake

The land that the Aztecs found was just a tiny island, surrounded by a lake. They employed a local farming method called *chinampa.* They created artificial islands in the lake by piling up mud and soil in the shallow lake bed. These islands looked like small, rectangular areas where the Aztecs could grow crops. According to Jorge, M et al., these measured at 30 m × 2.5 m and the Aztecs measured these beds in *matl* (one *matl* was equivalent to 1.67 m). First, they marked the limits of the soil bed by using stakes they pushed into the shallow lake bed. Next, they fenced it off in a rectangle, using a lightweight construction material called wattle. They made it by weaving thin branches together and tying them to upright stakes to form a woven lattice.

This was demanding work, but it paid off because the soil was incredibly fertile for planting crops. Although they were still paying tribute to the Tepanecs, in time, they could live on their land autonomously and grow crops. What's more, the area was defensible because it was perched in the middle of a lake and surrounded by water.

Life was still tough for the Aztecs. Jose Luis de Rojas, an anthropologist from the University of Madrid, wrote that "early years were difficult." People lived in huts, and even the temples dedicated to Huitzilopochtli were made of "perishable material." But day-by-day, their territory expanded until in 1325 they named their new city Tenochtitlán.

Chapter 3 – The Rise of Tenochtitlán and the Triple Alliance

"To give an account … of the greatness, and the strange and marvelous things of this great city of Tenochtitlán … and of all the dominions and splendor of Moctezuma its sovereign; of all the rites and customs which these people practice, and of the order prevailing in the government, not only of this city but also of others belonging to this lord, much time and many very expert narrators would be required."

This is what Hernando Cortés wrote to Holy Roman Emperor Charles V in 1520 regarding what he saw in the great Aztec city of

Tenochtitlán. It was a city built entirely on a lake, with canal transport systems, rivalled only by the Italian city of Venice. Beautiful temples adorned the streets of this great city, among them the Aztecs' greatest gem - the principal temple that, according to Cortés, could easily house an entire town of 500 inhabitants.

This was only 200 years after the Aztecs founded their great city. So how did Tenochtitlán rise from an uninhabited tiny island in the middle of a lake to the greatest and most splendid fortress that Mesoamerica had ever seen?

Let's visit 1325 again. The Aztecs paid tribute to the Tepanecs during this period. They helped the Tepanecs to conquer more land, achieving greater riches. As their wealth increased, so did the wealth of the Aztecs. But they were still not entirely free. However, in 1427 the Aztec leader Itzcoatl decided to take some bold and drastic steps to take control back. He forged a powerful alliance with two other city-states, Tetzcoco and Tlacopan, also known as the Triple Alliance. Together, they conquered the Tepanec rulers and their great wealth transferred to the Aztecs and their allies.

The Triple Alliance

When the three tribes (the Aztecs, Acolhua, and Tepanec) came together to create a triple alliance of their respective cities, it created a powerful military force. Eventually, the Aztecs used their cunning ways to sack their allies and become the dominant force in the entire region. Who knows how far their empire would have expanded, had it not been for the arrival of the Spanish conquistadors in the year 1519.

The Foundation of the Triple Alliance

Around 1350 AD, the region where the Aztecs dwelled was divided into small, centralized city-states, each with its own ruler and administrative centre. The city-states owned a surrounding area of smaller villages and hamlets that depended upon the city. Some of these cities fought each other, while others had friendlier relationships. They traded with each other and worshipped similar deities. Nonetheless, each wanted to be more powerful than the other.

After much bickering and trading, two city-states became the leaders of the region. These were Tlacopan, ruled by the Tepanecs, and Tetzcoco, home of the Acoulha tribe. At this point, the Aztecs were still paying taxes to the Tepanecs. But all that changed when another city-state, Azcapotzalco, entered the region in 1418.

As the power of Azcapotzalco increased, the Aztecs were forced to pay more tributes to them. Yet in the year 1428, the Aztecs joined their forces with Tetzcoco and finally revolted against their oppressors. This two-city alliance was gaining some important victories, and after they had proved their worth, the Tepanec city of Tlacopan decided it would be beneficial to join the alliance. This was the birth of the Triple Alliance, and together the three city-states defeated Azcapotzalco.

Confident in their achievements, the three city-states soon realised they could go much further. In 1473, they conquered the entire basin and ruled with an overwhelming military force.

Unequal Rights Within the Alliance

However, despite their quick success, the power within the Triple Alliance was not always equally distributed. Although each city still enjoyed complete political autonomy, the distribution of wealth and the spoils of war was unequal. Usually, an equal amount of the loot went to Tetzcoco and Tenochtitlán (each received ⅖ of the entire amount of goods) while only ⅕ went to Tlacopan, as this city was the last to join the alliance.

Over time, the cities became unequal in other aspects, too. Tenochtitlán later became the military leader, having the strongest army, while Tetzcoco lead in other spheres of life, such as law, engineering, and the arts, which the Aztecs greatly revered and held in high esteem.

Having different strengths allowed the cities to remain the dominant presence in the region, ruling together with their military force, political strategies, and their excellent, ever-expanding trade networks. The Triple Alliance was strengthened further with elite marriages between the noble families. The Triple Alliance grew economically too, as their client states had to pay them taxes in the form of products that freely entered the markets of the three city-states, ensuring a constant supply of trade.

How the Triple Alliance Disintegrated

Since Tenochtitlán was the military leader of the Alliance, its rulers soon realised they could make the final decisions on all military actions. The Aztec rulers began to disintegrate their allied states - first Tlacopan, then Tetzcoco.

They were less successful with the latter, and the city-state of Tetzcoco remained independent right up until the arrival of the Spanish. Although Tenochtitlán dominated the alliance, it continued to exist through political, social, and economic means, sharing the common goal of regional domination.

Tenochtitlán's arrogance eventually led to its downfall. Since Tetzcoco had grown hostile towards the alliance and the Aztecs, it later aided Hernando Cortés to overthrow this great city, succeeding in 1591.

Chapter 4 – The Greatest Aztec Kings and Their Heritage

Before we go on to examine all the wonders of the great Aztec city of Tenochtitlán as it would have stood when the Spanish conquistadors found it, let's first get an overview of the greatest Aztec rulers and their accomplishments.

It's important to mention another civilization that the Aztecs tried to emulate in everything they did.

The Toltec heritage

The Aztecs attempted to change their reputation of being savage foreigners. They tried to emulate the Toltec civilization, seen by many Mesoamerican cultures as one of the greatest civilizations that ever existed. Many tried to link their lineage to the Toltecs, who were seen as the supreme example of political leadership, artistic skill, and noble excellency. They were seen a bit like the legendary Atlantis is seen by the modern world - a splendid civilization destroyed by a terrible catastrophe, the origins of which still puzzle many archaeologists and historians to this day. But similar to Atlantis, not much evidence has been found of the existence of a Toltec civilization. Despite the Toltec cult that many Mesoamerican cultures displayed, could it have been nothing more than a myth?

The Aztecs adored the Toltecs - they were the supreme example of leadership and excellency that the Aztecs wanted to aspire to. They believed the Toltecs "taught the clay to lie" with their great artistic abilities. And it wasn't just the Aztecs. The Zapotecs, the Mayan civilization, and pretty much everyone across Mesoamerica loved the Toltecs, holding their civilization in the highest esteem.

The Aztec elite was among the most fervent emulators of the Toltecs. One of the greatest Toltec arts was the art of public speaking. In Náhuatl, the language that the Aztecs spoke, a king was called "Tlatoani" or "the one who speaks."

They also used the Toltec symbolism of eagles and jaguars frequently - it became a signature symbol for the Aztec art of war. Additionally, they built ball courts and skull racks and some very peculiar sacrificial statues, similar to those that the Toltecs had.

Is there any truth in the Toltec myth?

Despite this influence, there is little archaeological evidence found to support the myth of a Toltec civilization. There was a

Toltec nation, but their capital city of Tula could hardly be seen called the greatest cradle of Mesoamerican civilization. The city housed approximately 30,000 people during its peak between 900 and 1200 AD. It was surrounded by thousands of stone houses with flat roofs where extended families lived, all crammed together. They did have some workshops inside those houses, but they were simple and small - Tula never reached the great level of artistry that the Aztecs described. Similar to other Mesoamerican nations, the people at Tula had corn in every meal, and they had just enough food to feed their population.

Many archaeologists agree the Toltec empire has been massively overestimated. The Aztecs took steps to recast their own history, so their idealization of the Toltecs may have been spurred on by their propaganda at the time.

Now that we know exactly where the Aztecs had come from and whom they aspired to be let's take a quick look at their greatest kings and their most notable achievements.

Acamapichtli, The First Aztec Ruler (1375 - 1395)

Acamapichtli's name translates as "a handful of reeds." He was the first leader of the Aztecs (note that they did not have an empire yet). Originally from Tetzcoco, Acamapichtli was only 20 years old when he became the leader of the Aztecs, thanks to his ties with other important families and his bold claims to be a direct descendant of the Toltecs whom the Aztecs idealized.

He arrived in Tenochtitlán and was received with great ceremony. During the 19 years of his reign, Acamapichtli married several times (Aztec rulers could have more than one wife). To strengthen the strategic ties between the city, he married Ilancueitl, the daughter of the ruler of Culhuacán. He also married a wife from each of Tenochtitlán's four *calpullis,* or districts.

He expanded the city's farmland on the lake while trying to hold off the hostile Azcapotzalco forces, to whom Tenochtitlán paid tribute each year. The first Aztec laws emerged during his reign, along with stone houses that replaced houses made of cane and reeds. He was an excellent politician and managed to strengthen his position by remaining diplomatic and clever, rather than forceful.

Acamapichtli is believed to have founded the Great Pyramid or Templo Mayor of Tenochtitlán, an architectural wonder that would not be fully completed until 1487.

The reigns of Huitzilihuitl, Chimalpopoca, and Itzcóatl (1396 - 1440)

A depiction of Huitzilihuitl. Source:
https://en.wikipedia.org/wiki/Huitzilihuitl

Huitzilihuitl carried on with the clever trade negotiations started by his father. He married the daughter of the ruler of Azcapotzalco, whom the Aztecs still paid tribute to. His second wife gave birth to Moctezuma I, who would later succeed the throne. Huitzilihuitl built a port and vastly expanded the cotton trade. Later, he aided his father-in-law in his attempts to attack Tetzcoco and succeeded in sacking many important cities around the region. He died around 1417, succeeded by Chimalpopoca.

Chimalpopoca ruled Tenochtitlán for about nine years. The attempts to secure more control over the region by Azcapotzalco's rulers eventually led to Chimalpopoca's assassination and the exile of Tetzcoco's ruler. However, this sparked the idea of the Triple Alliance. Azcapotzalco's aggression led to talks between Itzcóatl, Chimalpopoca's successor, and the rulers of Tetzcoco and Tlacopan who worked together to form the Triple Alliance and defend themselves against Azcapotzalco. In 1428, their efforts succeeded and they conquered Atzcapotzalco.

Moctezuma I - the first ruler of the Aztec Empire (1440 - 1469)

Moctezuma I as depicted in Codex Mendoza.
Source:
https://en.wikipedia.org/wiki/Moctezuma_I

Moctezuma I was the son of Huitzilihuitl and the first king of Tenochtitlán who really represented the city's wealth, independence, and power. During his uncle Itzcóatl's reign, Moctezuma I became one of his strongest supporters. He is believed to have been a wise ruler and a fierce warrior and statesman. Thanks to his efforts, he created order, in the quickly growing Aztec empire while expanding its borders. His first successful war campaign was against the city of Chalco and was followed by many other victories.

However, Moctezuma had his fair share of troubles. A four-year drought that fell upon the region led to starvation among his people, and many of the Aztecs died. Other natural disasters, such as heavy snow, floods, and frost destroyed the crops. Nonetheless, he created order and restored Tenochtitlán's prosperity through his war efforts, trade links, and diplomatic negotiations.

Moctezuma I was a good leader in war. He was also a brilliant statesman, and he understood the need for advancement not only in his war efforts but in the education of his people. He wanted them to become more sophisticated, and have a stronger sense of an identity - he wanted his people to be proud of who they were and where they came from. He introduced many innovative ideas to his people. He ordered the rewriting of Aztec history and reworked the Aztec calendar. Moctezuma I was the one who organised an expedition to find the mythical land of Aztlán, from which the Mexica were believed to have emerged.

He was also an innovator. Moctezuma I brought a fresh water supply to the city and implemented important laws to keep order within the society. He also ordered the construction of fascinating sculptures, stunning temples, and beautiful botanical gardens.

He introduced a new tradition, called Guerra Florida or "The Wars of Flowers." These were ritual wars, fought between the members of the Triple Alliance and their enemies. The two armies would meet on an established date at an agreed location that would later become a sacred site. This meant a far lesser cost to either party than an actual war. The start of the war was announced by the burning of a pyre of paper and incense in between the two armies, which consisted of an equal number of participants. The use of different weapons was also restricted, and the Aztecs preferred to use weapons that would require a close proximity to their enemies.

Although the "Flower Wars" usually meant that fewer soldiers were needed for the battles, it was usually the nobles who fought in these wars. If they happened to die during such a battle, their death was considered especially precious, referred to as *xochimiquiztli*. According to American historian and anthropologist Ross Hassig, this can be translated as "flowery death," "blissful death," or "fortunate death."

Needless to say, Moctezuma I left behind a legacy that would help future Aztec kings build and expand their empire.

The reign of Axayacatl, Tizoc, and Ahuitzotl (1469 - 1502)

Moctezuma I was succeeded by Axayacatl, Itzcóatl's grandson, who was only 19 at the time. Since being a king was not a hereditary privilege in the Aztec world, Axayacatl was elected by the leaders of the Aztec empire and supported by the leaders of Tenochtitlán's allied city-states, Texcoco and Tacuba.

It must have been hard for Axayacatl to compete with the legacy of Moctezuma I, who had ruled the Aztec Empire for almost 30 years. The only way to excel was to build upon the previous ruler's success. Right before his coronation, Axayacatl led an expedition against the rebellious city of Cotaxtla. He brought back prisoners who were used as human sacrifices to the gods during his coronation ceremony.

During his reign, Axayacatl continued his line of work by expanding the Aztec empire through war efforts, diplomacy and trade, and constructing grand public buildings to make Tenochtitlán the most stupendous city in Mesoamerica. He conquered the cities of Toluca, parts of Malinalco and Matlatzinca, Tuxpan.

These victories culminated in his biggest war effort - subduing the Aztec allied city of Tlatelolco in 1473, despite his sister's marriage to its ruler Moquihuix. From then on, Tlatelolco was not permitted to have its own ruler.

However, under Axayacatl's reign, the Aztecs also suffered their biggest military defeat before the arrival of the Spanish. In 1478, he led a poorly planned war expedition against the Tarascans in Michoacan. The Aztecs were greatly outnumbered and suffered a great defeat, with only 200 men returning to Tenochtitlán, most of whom were wounded.

Axayacatl was only 30 when he died, but, in addition to his military exploits, he also ordered the construction of the final phase of the grand temple dedicated to the god Huitzilopochtli, as well as a temple dedicated to the rain god Tlaloc. He also ordered the Aztec calendar to be carved on a massive stone that allowed the Aztecs to measure the time with great precision.

He was succeeded by Tizoc, who ruled for only five years. From 1481 to 1486, he started some monumental projects, such as the rebuilding of the Great Pyramid of Tenochtitlán. According to the Codex of Mendoza, Tizoc conquered many city-states, among them Tonalimoquetzayan, Toxico, Ecatepec, Cillán, Tecaxic, Tolocan, Yancuitlan, Tlappan, Atezcahuacan, Mazatlán, Xochiyetla, Tamapachco, Ecatliquapechco, and Miquetlan. He died of unknown causes - some speculate that he was poisoned while others claim that he died of a deadly illness.

Tizoc was succeeded by Ahuitzotl, the last *tlatoani* before Moctezuma II took the throne. He is remembered as one of the greatest military leaders of Pre-Columbian Mesoamerica. Shortly after his crowning ceremony, he doubled the size of the Aztec empire, conquering the Zapotec, the Mixtec, and many other Mesoamerican tribes. He also expanded the Great Pyramid and the Templo Mayor.

Among some of his most interesting achievements is the successful introduction of a bird species known as the great-tailed grackle into the Valley of Mexico.

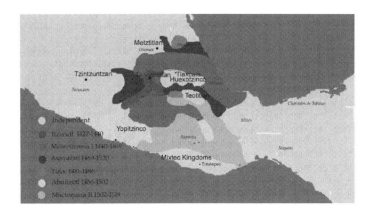

This map shows the expansion of the Aztec empire with each successive ruler. Source: https://en.wikipedia.org/wiki/Ahuitzotl

Chapter 5 – The Splendor of Tenochtitlán

The ancient Aztec city of Tenochtitlán was truly spectacular. It did not have a rival in all of Mesoamerica, quickly becoming known as the capital of the New World. At the time, Paris only had 150,000 inhabitants, whereas Tenochtitlán housed 200,000 with around 50,000 people attending the bustling market stalls every day.

The construction of Tenochtitlán and its rise to become a successful and bustling city is a testimony to what can be achieved with hard work and ingenuity. By combining the two, it took the Aztecs only two years to turn the tiny island in the middle of Lake Texcoco into the capital of the New World.

Europe could not compete with the sophistication of the city, with its water aqueducts, zoos, and exotic gardens. When the Spanish Conquistadors, led by Hernando Cortés, first set foot on the land of Tenochtitlán in November 1519, it was like nothing they'd ever seen before. Nothing could match either the splendor of the city nor its thirst for human sacrifice.

The Aztec world needs to be viewed through two seemingly opposing lenses. One is their reverence for the arts, poetry, music, and beauty. The other is their love of human sacrifice. Thousands of people were sacrificed in the many temples across Tenochtitlán every year, and this went hand-in-hand with their more palatable religious rites and rituals.

Social order

There were several social castes in the Aztec world, and the higher you were, the more privileges you could enjoy. However, in higher castes, the social norms you had to obey were stricter.

The life of a slave in the Aztec world

Slaves were bought and sold daily in the central market place. They had a designated area, like the other merchants like potters or jewellers. Slaves were at the very bottom of the social order, but they did have some rights. Anyone could end up a slave. If you didn't pay your debts or gambled too much, if you were a foreign captive or if you committed crimes, you might become a slave to pay your dues. Some people sold themselves into slavery to rid themselves of debts or families sometimes sold their children so they could support the rest of the family.

Slave owners had an obligation to feed and house their slaves. The slave's loss of freedom was reported in official documents and decrees.

Your fortune as a slave depended on who purchased you. Because you couldn't decide who that would be, you'd likely pray you were bought by a noble who wanted you to be their servant. Unfortunately for some slaves, priests could also buy slaves specifically for sacrifice. But many noble houses had slaves as servants, and they could live comfortable lives. They could even have time off and earn some money. They could marry and have children, and their children were not considered slaves but free men. Thus slavery was not considered hereditary.

The life of a commoner

This was the biggest social class in the ancient Aztec world, making up about 95% of the population. Most commoners were farmers (who usually tended the land that belonged to the nobles) or craftsmen who did pottery or woodwork, among other trades. Some of them were also soldiers, but all Aztec men were warriors at heart. They had to complete military service for the Aztec army as part of their obligations, and all boys, commoners, and nobles, started learning the art of war from a young age.

As in most ancient societies, fate was very different for women. They were expected to stay at home, doing textiles, cleaning the house, and cooking for the family. They were also the most frequent visitors to the nearby markets.

The families of commoners lived in one-room houses that were made of reed walls and wattle. There were no windows and only one door. They slept on simple reed mats and had a hearth inside that kept them warm during cold nights. Children stayed at home to learn the trade of their parents or they went to school as early as age five (only boys).

They lived like this in tiny districts, where four or five families, usually blood-related, shared the same patio. Each of these areas had a *temazcal* (a type of a sweat bath or lodge that translates as "house of heat"). Children were often born inside the *temazcal.*

Each noble usually ruled over a neighbourhood of commoners who belonged to them. The noble would assign labour in that neighbourhood, and they had a small palace inside the neighbourhood. There would also be a temple and a school for children to attend free of charge, and sometimes even a small ball court for the famous Rubber Ballgame that was popular across Mesoamerica.

The middle class and travelling merchants

The Aztec middle class was made up of travelling merchants. But they were much more than just traders of exotic goods. The merchants served the king himself as diplomats or spies, who assessed if new lands were suitable for conquest while away on their missions, which could last several months at a time. It was a dangerous vocation, and they were all trained warriors who carried weapons on them. They hired professional carriers to come along with them on their missions, who were also trained warriors.

There were relatively few merchants around - only 12 merchant guilds existed in Tenochtitlán - and you could only become a merchant by being born into a merchant family. Thus, commoners could not aspire to become merchants. Despite the great wealth the merchants accumulated following their successful trade missions, they could not actively display that wealth. Often, they dressed in rags upon return, because only nobles could dress in expensive capes and wear jewellery that displayed their social status.

The merchants too had social responsibilities - they were also the judges of the markets where the buying and selling of their goods took place, settling disputes among the visitors and stallholders.

The Nobles

The nobles constituted only 5% of the entire population, and commoners or merchants could not aspire to become a noble. Along with the king, they owned Aztec land, and their children were sent to special schools. Whereas the schools for commoners taught the art of war only, these schools would train children in poetry, public speaking, the calendric system, and many other arts and skills the Aztecs held in high esteem. Children leaving these schools were destined to become government officials, high priests, and captains in the Aztec army.

They lived in spacious palaces with stone walls and cedar beams. Whereas the commoners did not have much in their house at all, these nobles enjoyed finely crafted furniture and ate from beautiful plates, allocating many beautiful rooms to their many servants.

They were expected to be model citizens and illuminate the way for the rest. If they misbehaved in any way and broke the social norms, the punishment was more severe than that reserved for commoners who'd committed the same crime. They also had to be more proactive in their social obligations towards the public, organising public feasts, leading labour teams, as well as leading armies.

The King and High Priest

The king was at the very top of the Aztec social hierarchy. The role of the king was not hereditary - even if an Aztec king was your father, you still had to be elected by a group of nobles to become the next ruler. Thus, your status was always based on your merit or how well you'd appeased the nobles. Although a king had his advisors, he would oversee everything from daily sacrifices, to battle and political strategies, as well as negotiations with foreign kings. The king was the father figure of the nation, as well as their spiritual leader, and thus had to set an excellent example.

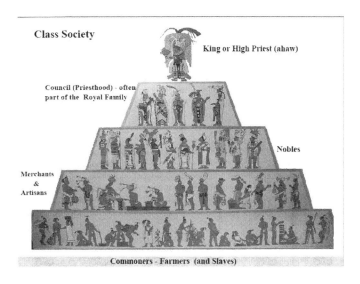

Aztec social order. Source *https://aztecprojectempire.files.wordpress.com/20* *12/11/social-pyramid.png*

Take a walk in the king's shoes

If you were Moctezuma II, you might wake up in your breathtaking and spacious bedroom, possibly next to one of your many beautiful wives.

One of the thousands of servants would help you get dressed. Cleanliness was an important virtue in the Aztec civilization, so you'd wash frequently. After having some breakfast, you'd attend to important stately business. As you wandered through the hundreds of rooms that were reserved for visiting nobles and ambassadors, each with a private en-suite bathroom, on one of the top palace floors, you might catch a glimpse of the priest precinct that was situated right next to the palace, where human sacrifice was part of everyday life. As the head of the state, you'd personally oversee some of them and consult with the high priests to make sure that these rituals were carried out in accordance to the whims of the gods. You probably wouldn't notice how strange it might have appeared to have such beauty and savagery exist right next to each other.

You'd adore the beautiful handcrafted tapestries and murals that adorned the walls, observing good graces by greeting the people you encounter. Hundreds of servants and slaves would emerge from their rooms, ready to attend to your every need. You'd be formal but kind to them, and generous from time to time, as the warm but firm father figure and spiritual leader that you were expected to be.

After you'd walked for what seemed like forever, you'd finally get to the bottom floor, ready for an important meeting. There was never a shortage of them, as being the owner of all the lands in the city and the taxes paid, a lot rested on your shoulders. As well as overseeing the daily sacrifices, you'd be responsible deciding on all the political and battle strategies. Besides, you'd want to keep those nobles who elected you pleased.

You may have to struggle a bit to get through all the gifts piled on the bottom floor from lords and rich visitors who wanted to pay tribute to you and your powerful empire. It wouldn't be unusual if a king from another city had come down to visit you - they had to forge their own political strategies.

Later in the evening, you'd get dressed in your finest clothes, colourfully embroidered and decorated with feathers (the more, the better). You would make your way downstairs for the daily feast, where you'd welcome the new visitor who'd arrived at your palace. You'd want to show off your empire and exhibit good graces to them, so you'd welcome them at your table. It wouldn't be just the two of you though. 300 plates would be on your table alone, all kept warm using a special heating technique, then piled with delicious food from the local market. As soon as you touched any of it, a woman would rush by your side to wash your hands while you enjoyed the festivities and the merriment provided by the many singers, jesters, and dwarfs who were highly esteemed in your country.

Once the feast was finished, you'd leave the room, allowing the hundreds of guards and servants who helped prepare the meal to have their share in the same dining hall. Having cleansed yourself again, you'd go to bed, fast asleep, without the slightest idea that a few centuries later the grand palace you inhabited would lie in ruins, buried under another beautiful building called The National Palace in Mexico City.

Chapter 6 - A Guided Tour Around Tenochtitlán

Let's now take a walk around the rest of the city, parts of which the king would have been able to see through his many, many palace windows.

We have a choice before us - we can travel in a canoe, across the city's many canals (just like people do in Venice). Merchants transported their goods around the city using the canals. Farmers used canoes to get to the lake surrounding the city and to drain the water for planting more crops in the murky waters.

Or we can do something more familiar and simply take a stroll on the ground. Since piloting a canoe might take some training, let's resort to getting around on our feet, something we're much more familiar with.

Tenochtitlán. Source: https://matadornetwork.com/es/solucion-inundaciones-tenochtitlan/

"Gather for the Official Tour of Tenochtitlán!," you hear a local tour guide shout, waving a feathered pole in his hand. "Come along and discover wonders that you would not encounter even in Europe!"

- Moctezuma II's Palace and his botanical gardens, housing every plant found in Mesoamerica;
- The zoo with the cat-house;
- The aquarium with every exotic fish that lives in the waters near and far;
- The Museum of Ancient Cultures;
- The Public Theatre where people 'dance with their feet;'
- The grand Templo Mayor (or, as you people like to call it, the Great Pyramid of Tenochtitlán).

"And last but by no means least, you'll see with your own eyes the biggest market that anyone has ever seen in all of Mesoamerica, with 50,000 people trading daily! They tell me it's bigger than your modern-day city of London! So, gather and prepare to be amazed!"

In awe, you and the others in your tour group follow the guide as he leads you through the city. It's going to be a long day, filled with adventure and wonder. You'll be gripped by both awe and terror as you unravel the wonders of this city, along with its gruesome tradition of human sacrifice.

The tour begins

You learn the entire city is divided into four major zones called *camps.* Each zone is further divided into twenty districts, commonly known as *calpullis.* Each of these *calpullis* had its own tribe or bloodline living there, with a separate marketplace, temple, and school.

Starting with the least impressive sights to build the tour to a crescendo, your local guide leads you inside one of the city's poorer *calpullis,* where farmers live. You see people emerge from simple huts with thatched roofs, rubbing sleep out of their eyes, wearing little clothing, almost ready to start their day. One of them, a man with coal-dark hair and dark skin that's been scorched in the sun, pops over to tend to his vegetable patch in the garden beside his house. He doesn't even wave hello to you, too preoccupied with the daily grind of his life.

"They can grow food for themselves here," the tour guide explains, after saying something to the man, to which he receives a crabby grunt in reply. You notice that the poor man doesn't have any feathers in the simple garments he's wearing - only nobles could wear feathers, as a sign of class and status.

You're taken aback as a string of children rush out from the same hut, boys and girls ranging from ages of five to fifteen. You wonder how they all fit inside the small hut, but they're all neatly dressed, in poor but clean garments. You ask the tour guide about them.

"They're off to school. Each neighbourhood of the poor has their own market, temple, and school. Girls have a different school to boys, but they all learn the laws and codes of behaviour because they know, even at this early age, that disobeying the law could mean death. That's why it's so important for them to learn this, and to do what society expects of them. Once they reach the age of fifteen, they get separated. The boys go on to learn important skills like hunting, farming, and fighting. The girls stay at home and learn sewing, how to be good mothers and cooks..."

The guide stops half-way, interrupted by a sudden noise. It sounded like a splash, as though something had been thrown in the water. You rush over to the scene, to find people laughing and cheering at a person swimming in the canal. The guide soon joins them.

"It's his birthday today," he explains. "This man was born on the day of air, not a good sign. It means he's destined to be lazy and a drifter. I myself was born on the day of the lizard. It means that I'm destined to become rich. Well, I'm still waiting for that day…"

You learn that this is a typical birthday celebration - friends wake you up by tossing you into a river and later you're obliged to throw them a party where you thank them and everyone who's helped you get to where you are. You ask the guide what would happen to the man if he couldn't afford to throw a feast?

"Well, then he'd be scorned for the rest of the year," he's quick to explain as you leave the scene and carry on with the tour.

Walking along the city's giant causeways

You're excited to see a house where a noble lives - you've heard of how rich and spectacular these could be, and you want to see it with your own eyes. You emerge from the *calpulli* and arrive on one of the three main streets that cross the city, each leading to one of the city's three causeways that connect Tenochtitlán to the mainland of Tepeyac, Ixtapalpa, and Tlacopan.

As you step onto one of the causeways, you're amazed at how accurate one of the Spanish conquistadors, Bernal Díaz was in his autobiographical account, *The Conquest of New Spain.* He said that each causeway was wide enough to fit ten horses, and it really is that huge! They had to be to sustain all the commerce and visitors arriving and leaving the city daily.

"Over there." The guide points in the distance while you wait for one of the draw-bridges to lift and let a boat pass through underneath before you can carry on with your journey. These were also lifted in times of siege when the land needed to be defended, severing mainland access to the city. "Over there is the great Aztec market. It's in the sister city Tlatelolco. The city was established in 1358 and ruled by a Tepanec prince at that time. It became part of Tenochtitlán only in 1473."

In the distance, you can also see lots of tiny islands surrounding the city - they look more like blobs from where you're standing, with ant-like creatures walking around. Those are the farmers, the guide explains, noticing your puzzled gaze. He points to one of the islands. "That's the man we met this morning. He's planting food and flowers using chinampas. We, the Aztec people, are very proud that we can grow everything we need in Tenochtitlán. We can grow our own food and raise our own army. The lake protects us against invaders, and the fertile soil protects our food supply. That's how we started really. We used chinampas, piling mud and muck on top of reed structures, laying low until 1427, when the beautiful part of our city began to emerge. I will show you all of our gems later in the tour."

A model of the Templo Mayor precinct. Source *http://www.ancient.eu/image/1440/*

It's hard to miss the most impressive structure in all Tenochtitlán, as it rises so high it almost clouds the sun. Again, the guide is quick to notice your gaze, and he fills in the blanks in your mind.

"This is our Great Temple or Templo Mayor. In fact, let's go there next, before we visit the nobles' houses, as I'm sure you'll be too preoccupied with its grand structure to focus on anything else."

As you walk the streets, trying to shield yourself from the scorching heat of the sun, you can't help but be amazed at the impressive engineering knowledge that the Aztecs had.

"See all these canals, they actually ensure that the water never grows stale in the lake. It keeps on moving and flowing, so it's always fresh and replenished. One of our great nobles built 16 km worth of walls around the city, to separate the brackish water from the rest of the lake."

He points at a pipe running along the canals and causeways like a giant snake. "Every house has access to tap water - fresh, running water that comes straight from the lake, transported via two massive stone and terracotta pipes via the aqueducts. The pipes go all the way to Chapultepec hill 4 km away. In case you're wondering why we have two pipes, it's to ensure that we always have a working pipe when the other one needs to be cleaned. We Aztecs take great pride in cleanliness, it's a sign of good manners and class."

You ask the guide if you could get a drink of water because the sun is so hot. He says the water in the taps is not potable. He stops at one of the smaller markets on the way and shows you a stall that sells bottled water. You swallow the water thirstily, amazed the ancient Aztecs were drinking bottled water from the nearby springs.

Inside the Temple Mayor precinct

And finally, you've arrived. Templo Mayor is there, right in the middle where all the city's districts meet. You look up, but you can't seem to see the end to its two main towers, accessed by a massive flight of stairs. You know from reading guide books that the pyramid is 60m tall, and stands on a platform of four tiers. Two flights of steps lead up towards its entrance, the western side leading to a summit where two twin temples glisten in the sun, the entire structure painted in bright colours over lime plaster. One is red and the other blue, each representing the colours of a different god.

How tall was Templo Mayor?

The height of Templo Mayor would be equivalent to:

- 14 double-decker buses, stacked on top of each other.
- 8.5 three-story houses.
- a hotel or residential home with 16 stories.

You come back from your daydream, and hear the guide's voice again, loud, and clear, wondering what interesting facts you've missed while you calculated the height of Templo Mayor.

"The Temple is symbolic of Cayutopec: it was built on the very spot where they saw the sign of the cactus, symbolizing the birthplace of their god.

"You're standing at the exact spot where our great god Huitzilopochtli gave his great sign for us, the people of Mexica. This is where our elders saw a cactus with an eagle perched on top, holding a snake in its mouth."

You must wonder if this is what really happened, or if it is just an elaborate fairytale that gave the Aztecs the right to claim the island on the lake.

"We have dedicated our great temple to our war god Huitzilopochtli and our rain god Tlaloc. We thank them for blessing us with a good fortune and keep them appeased by providing regular human sacrifice."

Somewhere in the distance, you feel like you can hear a faint echo of a scream. A woman, a slave or a child perhaps? You came on the tour, mentally prepared for this, but you can't help but shudder.

"Each god has their own requirements," the guide carries on. "Sometimes we need to get children, sometimes foreigners, sometimes people who are willing to be sacrificed, earning themselves honour."

You try to keep calm, suddenly startled by the realisation that although you are a visitor here, you are nonetheless a foreigner.

The guide lines up your group in front of the giant steps and explains more about the temple. "It's taken many lifetimes to build. Our great king Itzcoatl ordered the construction of the temple around 1427 to 1440. Moctezuma I and his successor Ahuitzotl made further improvements, wanting to top their predecessors."

"Today, this temple is what you might call the social and religious centre of our culture. If you stood at the top of the sacred Processional Way during summer equinox, you'd see the sun rising between the two shrines of the upper platform. That's how precise our astronomers and builders were when constructing it."

The guide looks down and instructs you to look around you, while he explains that the entire precinct is 365m wide on each side, surrounded by a wall. "We call it the 'Serpent Wall' because of the snake relief carvings that you can see on the walls."

You take a closer look and run your fingers against the relief on the wall. You are amazed by the detail all along the wall, and as you look around, you try to count how many other buildings are in the precinct, enclosed by its tall walls. You get to 78, when you realise you've drifted off again.

Until now, you've been trying to ignore the wall of skulls at the base of the pyramid, composed of thousands of skulls from sacrificial victims. You're not sure if you want to hear any more detail on this, so you don't ask the guide.

Your attention is suddenly caught by something else - a drunk young man stumbles inside the precinct, pushed along by two heavily armed Aztec guards.

The guide watches him with contempt. "He's a local potter," he says. "Certainly, no noble, but I've seen his stuff being sold at the markets. What a shame that he's given into drinking."

The guards lead him away towards the temple where priests already await them. The man seems so delirious with drink that he does not understand what's going on. Maybe it's for the best.

You tentatively ask the tour guide what will happen to the young man. "He should know better the laws and rules of our society. Lucky for him, he'll be sacrificed to the gods, his body stretched out on a large stone on the top of the pyramid, while a priest slabs an obsidian knife right into his chest and rips his heart out as an offering to the gods."

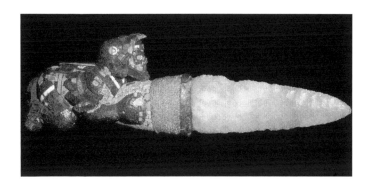

Aztec sacrificial knife. Source:
https://www.thoughtco.com/aztec-triple-alliance-
170036

The guide tells all this without blinking. Equally calm, he carries on.

"Then he'll be dismembered and decapitated, and what remains of him will be tossed down the steps of the pyramid to land at the base. His fate will be the same as the goddess Coyolxauhqui, who tried to defy our great god Huitzilopochtli."

All this for being drunk, you think to yourself, and decide to watch your alcohol intake at the Aztec feast tonight. You wonder if you should say something, step ahead and defend the young man who simply made a mistake. But you remember how the Aztecs called Hernan Cortes evil, after he criticized their practices, and told him never to say those words again. You remind yourself of the size of the Aztec army and realise that there is nothing you can do, except forget what happened here.

You leave the precinct and Templo Mayor with a knot in your stomach, feeling nauseous. The temple's splendour is overshadowed by what you've learned of Aztec human sacrifices. From reading the guidebooks, you know that thousands of people - somewhere between 10,000 to 80,000, the sources disagree - were sacrificed here on the 7th phase of the temple's inauguration. Either way, the priests had their hands covered in blood for three days. It's hard to imagine that today Mexico City's main plaza stands here.

You wonder how the Spanish conquistadors felt, when they first arrived in the city, amazed by all its wonder and beauty, while disgusted at its brutal practices. But those are the Aztecs; you remind yourself. For all their beauty and love of art, they'll always remain warriors at heart.

Next stop - the zoo!

You're happy to hear that you'll be visiting something more light-hearted next - the city's zoo and its aquarium. From reading, you know that this truly astonished the Spanish conquistadors, who had never seen anything like this before.

First, you're taken to the zoo. By special arrangement, you're granted access to Moctezuma II's castle again, where the zoo is located for his entertainment. You watch many of the 300 zookeepers busy themselves around large and scary animals you've never seen before and, like the Spanish conquistadors, are not able to name, except to say they look like lions.

However, you do recognize some animals that were described by the Franciscan monk Bernardino de Sahagún in the vast, encyclopedic body of work that he created on Aztec customs, rites, and history in the 16th century. Although the church was quick to confiscate much of the material upon his return to Europe, much has survived in a document called the Florentine Codex. Among these are ocelots, bears, some mountain lions, and even eagles. In fact, there's a vast section dedicated specifically to birds of prey, and it looks like the zookeepers are having a hard time keeping them tamed. There's also reptiles, deer, different types of dogs, jaguars, turtles, and rattle-snakes, whom the Spanish conquistadors referred to as "snakes with music in their tails."

It would require an entire day to really appreciate all the animals, and you've got plenty more to see, so the tour guide ushers you on.

Since you're here, the tour guide explains it would be a pity to miss a tour of the botanical gardens also found in Moctezuma II's castle.

The Botanical Gardens

You've already been awestruck by the many gardens you've come across on your walk around the city, by their beauty and arrangements, as well as how well tended they are by the city's many gardeners.

But the Botanical Garden of Tenochtitlán is simply something else. You've never seen such a variety of plants. For the Aztecs, flowers symbolized everything from life to death, from creation to destruction, from friendship to loneliness. Flowers were important, and this was certainly noticeable throughout the botanical garden. In fact, this practice would later inspire botanical gardens all over Europe.

"The botanical garden of Moctezuma II's palace and those established in the king's other residencies are one of a kind," the tour guide explains. "They have hundreds of unique plant species, looked after by specialist gardeners, and if one of the species withers or dies, then an entire expedition is sent out into the lands beyond Tenochtitlán to fetch another sample."

It's certainly impressive, but the aquarium leaves an even bigger impression on you.

The Aquarium and the Museum

A totally novel idea in Europe at the time, ten ponds of salt water and ten ponds of fresh water make up the aquarium. All kinds of fish swim happily around in both. The tour guide leaves the look and structure of these aquariums to your imaginations since not much evidence has remained about them.

You are taken by surprise when the tour guide takes you inside The Museum of Ancient Cultures next. You wander around the building, looking at various artefacts that the Aztecs had collected, many of them believed to be of Toltec and Olmec origin. You're amazed how familiar this feels to visits to your local museums back in the familiar environment of the 21st-century Western world.

The great Aztec jewel - Tlatelolco market

"I hope you are all ready for the final part of the tour. I have saved the best for last, so follow me to the greatest market Mesoamerica and perhaps the entire world has seen until now!"

The tour guide announces, and you set off on your journey to Tlatelolco, the sister city of Tenochtitlan. You encounter street sweepers and gardeners along the way, who seem to be going to great lengths to ensure that the city remains clean and tidy.

At the entrance to the great market, you notice an old man shouting abuse at the people walking past him. Despite his insults, people don't seem to be taking much notice of him. He is clearly drunk, waving a bottle in his hand as he gestures at the other people.

Soon, another old man joins him, and together they start dancing around the square like two fools.

Although your first impressions of these men create a strong dislike for them, you can't help but worry about them at the same time. You remember the punishment of the younger man who was drunk, and you worry that the same will happen to the two old men.

"What's going to happen to them?" You ask the tour guide, with doom on your face. You're not sure that you really want to hear the answer.

"What do you mean?" The tour guide looks puzzled.

You voice your concerns about the punishment awaiting them and the tour guide bursts out in hysterical laughter. All eyes are suddenly on you, and suddenly you are afraid of your own fate.

"I've never heard such a thing in my life!" The tour guide says, wiping tears from his eyes. Firstly, he's shocked that you're still thinking about what happened to the young man. Second, he explains that old men in the Aztec world are like gods - they have completed their duties to their elders and raised their children, so they can do whatever they wish and no one bats an eyelid.

You soon forget the incident as the tour guide leads you inside the markets, a sight you'll truly never forget.

Inside the markets

Life is bustling inside the markets, and your eyes dart from stall to stall, from item to item. Everything from pottery to cloth, gold, jewellery, and even slaves are sold.

The tour guide points towards a panel of judges who are settling disputes. To the left of you, a pickpocket is being arrested for trying to steal a jade jewel from one of the stalls. Across from him, a woman has her fortune read while she waits for her husband's hair to be cut.

Opposite you, all kinds of restaurants serve food from all over Mesoamerica. You suddenly notice how hungry you are, so you walk over to one of the stalls to buy some goodies. You sink your teeth inside a freshly baked maize tortilla and a fresh and incredibly ripe roasted avocado. You ask for a cup of Aztec cacao to wash it all down, and it's more bitter and spicy than you had imagined.

While you eat and chat to your fellow tour mates, you watch the Aztec families around you enjoy the performances from dancers, singers, and jugglers balancing logs on their feet as they lay down. You realise the markets are more than just a centre for commerce. For the Aztecs, it's a place for family outings, for catching up on the latest gossip, for taking a break from their duties or work. It is a place to come and be merry. As you stand in the marketplace, watching the various buyers and traders engage with each other, you realise you are standing right in the middle of the beating heart of the Aztec world.

Chapter 7 – Rites, Rituals, and Delicious Recipes

The Aztec calendar relied on a strict set of rules and social restrictions, enforced by law and religious festivities that took place throughout the year, designed to honour the gods, and bring the community together. In this section, you'll learn all about the calendar that directed the execution of some wonderful and some pretty horrific rituals that were intended to keep the gods happy. You'll also look at the typical duties that people in Aztec society had to carry out in their life and try your hand at some delicious Aztec food recipes. Prepare for a fun but gruesome journey!

The Aztec calendar

The Aztec calendar was based on astrological observations of the passage of the Sun, the Moon, and the planets. There was not only one calendar, but two!

1. The 'xiuhpohualli' had 365 days and described the days and rituals relating to the change in seasons. It could also be referred to as the agricultural calendar.

2. The 'tonalpohualli' translates into 'day-count,' and it had only 260 days. It was more commonly known as the sacred calendar.

In everyday life, the Aztec year comprised of 18 months of 20 days each that made up the 'xiuhpohualli' calendar. In addition, there were five 'useless days' called *Nemontemi* when people fasted, abstaining from sexual activities and pleasure. These were also the days when people engaged in voluntary bloodletting to appease the gods.

The calendar was at the heart of the Aztec festivities and events. Many of these are known to us, thanks to the efforts of Diego Durán, a Dominican friar who was born in Spain but arrived in Mexico in the 1540s while he was still a child. As a result, he grew up playing with the Aztec kids and befriended their families who shared more with him than they did with the other priests towards whom they were hostile.

He wrote his three books (one on Aztec history, one on their gods and rites, and another on the ancient calendar) in a desperate attempt to open the eyes of the other priests who funded religious activities in Aztec society. They had no idea that many brutal sacrifices still took place in secret, disguised as the Christian celebrations of the saints. Durán recorded these in detail, upset by most of them. Nonetheless, some of these festivities were rather nice and joyful, bringing the community closer together in a collective celebration.

For example, the first day of each month was a feast day. What's more, each day that started with number '1' in front of it was a day when all the people born under that sign were honoured. If the first day of the month happened to be the day of crocodile, then everyone who was named after the crocodile was honoured on that day.

This is what the Aztec calendar looked like, calculated in Durán's time.

Month and Description	Symbol
Atlcahualo, Cuauhitlehua March 1 - 20 Translation: Ceasing of Water,	

Rising Trees During this month, the Aztec people went around touching plants and offering food for gods, symbolic of them asking for a fruitful year.	
Tlacaxipehualiztli March 21 - April 9 Translation: Rites of Fertility The start of this month marked the spring equinox. One of the most gruesome Aztec rituals took place during this month, in honour of the god Xipe Totec. Captured warriors were sacrificed, their skin flayed and worn by the priests of Xipe Totec for 20 days. Children ran after the priests, playfully hitting them with their wooden	

toy swords. Gladiatorial battles and military ceremonies also took place during this month.	
Tozoztontli April 10 - 29 Translation: Little Vigil Several gods were honoured during this month with human sacrifices and offerings of flowers. The deities honoured during this month included Tlaloc, Coatlicue, Chalchihutlicue, and Centeotl. The flayed skins that the priests had worn during the previous month were buried in the Yopico temple.	
Huey Tozoztli April 30 - May 19 Translation: Great Vigil	

Several gods were honored during this month. These include Centeotl, Chalchiuhtlicue, Xilonen, Chicomecoatl, and Tlaloc.

Human sacrifices were rampant again, including child sacrifices and the sacrifice of a maiden as an offering to the corn and earth deities. People worshipped the new corn and asked for blessings over the seed of corn for that year. Houses and altars everywhere were decorated with corn plants. People and priests also engaged in ceremonial bloodletting, as they did during some of the other months.

Toxcatl

May 20 - June 8

Translation: Dryness

During this month, the Aztecs engaged in perhaps one of their most bizarre rituals. They chose one person from their midst to represent Tezcatlipoca, the god of fate and destiny. This person would be treated like a god, representing Tezcatlipoca until the day of his sacrifice. During the 17 days of this ceremony, people danced and feasted. The festivities culminated with the sacrifice of the fake Tezcatlipoca, along with small birds.

Etzalcualiztli

June 9 - 28

Translation: Eating Maize and Beans

This month pretty much did what it says on the tin - people feasted by eating boiled maize and beans during this month's festivities. The celebrations were dedicated to Tlaloc and Chalchiuhtlicue. But the merry festivities were not without their gruesome sacrifices. According to some chronicles, 15 children were sacrificed in the mountains, while others state people who impersonated the god Tlaloc and his wife cohabited for 20 days before they were sacrificed at midnight.

Tecuilhuitontli
June 29 - July 18
Translation: Feast for the
Revered Ones

The seventh month in the
Aztec calendar celebrated the
work of the salt makers and
the common folk who were
commemorated by the nobles
who hosted great festivities in
their honour. The concubines
of the nobles could leave their
houses and walk along the
streets with flower crowns on
their heads. The Great Speaker
would perform a dance in the
public and distribute gifts
among people. The saltmakers
had to dance too - they spent
ten entire days, dancing in

pairs, holding the end of a robe and singing in a high-pitched tone. The two main gods honored during this month were Xochipilli and Huixtocihuatl.

Huey Tecuilhuitl
July 19 - August 7
Translation: Feast for the Greatly Revered Ones

During this month, corn was usually ripe. Among the festivities, some gruesome sacrifices took place. A virgin was sacrificed during this month, lying on top of four men who made a kind of a table that supported her, before they were sacrificed

too.	
Miccailhuitontli August 8 - 27 Translation: Feast to the Revered Deceased The goddess Mictecacihuatl, or their Lady of the Dead, presided over this month, dedicated to children and the dead. People engaged in joyful festivities and feasting to remember their children and their ancestors who had passed away, and to honor Mictecacihuatl. Food items and small clay figurines or images of the deceased were brought to the altars as an offering.	

Xócotl huetzi, Huey Miccailhuitl August 28 - September 16 Translation: Feast to the Greatly Revered Deceased Continuing the theme of the previous month, the Aztec continued to honour their dead during this month.	
Ochpaniztli September 17 - October 6 Translation: Sweeping and Cleaning This was the month when the grandmother was honoured everywhere. It was also the month of cleaning and sweeping streets, houses, even rivers and streams, similar to	

our Western practices of 'spring cleaning.' However, Durán had his doubts - he believed that this month encouraged people to be sloths and neglect cleansing practices for the rest of the year.

Teotleco
October 7 - 26
Translation: Return of the Gods

On the 12th day of this month, the Aztec people spent the entire night waiting on the priests to announce the birth of their main god. They awaited the birth by practicing severe blood-letting and self-mutilation. When the birth was finally announced, everyone joined in a party, where people cut themselves and, caught in a daze of euphoria, rubbed blood all over each other.

Tepeilhuitl
October 27 - November 15
Translation: Feast of the Mountains

During this month, people honoured the volcanoes all around them, especially Popocatepetl. The Aztecs made tiny volcanoes from gemstones and painted faces on them. They honoured the volcanoes with a grand feast and finished the day by chopping off the

head of the volcano figurine using a sharp knife.	
Quecholli November 16 - December 5 Translation: Precious Feather One of the four creator gods in the Aztec pantheon was honoured. His name was Mixcoatl, otherwise known as the Cloud Serpent. Associated with the morning star, he also represented the hunt, having features of a deer or rabbit. Thus, a ceremonial hunt marked the festivities during this month. The last day of this month was also the day when the Aztecs made new weapons.	

Panquetzaliztli

December 6 - December 25

Translation: Raising the Banners

The fifteenth month of the Aztec calendar marked the Winter Solstice that occurred on 21 December. This was an incredibly important day, and preparations were carried out for the entire month. During this month, people decorated their houses with paper flags and trees, similarly to our preparations for Christmas festivities. Except the Aztecs also engaged in human sacrifice, among ritual races, dances, prayers, songs, and processions. People ate little during this month. At the end of the month though, an edible figurine of one of their gods, made of amaranth seeds and honey, was cut into pieces so that everyone could eat their share of the god.

Atemoztli
December 26 - January 14
Translation: Descent of the Water

Four days of bloodletting preceded this month, along with a strict fast. The festivities and rituals performed during this month aimed to appease Tlaloc, the Aztec god of water, to send waters down to earth, so they would help sow the season's new corn. The feast held in honour of Tlaloc was attended by the nobles (chiefs and lords). Corresponding rituals that were performed during this month include the sacrifice of slaves in the hills, the drowning of children to appease the rain god, and some gentler rituals, such as offerings of feathers.

Tititl

January 15 - February 12

Translation: Stretching for Growth

The planting season began during this month. People only ate amaranth leaves with their usual staple food, corn, as these had a special symbolism. The Aztecs also stretched the arms and legs of their children to promote growth. Typically, a boy and a girl were sacrificed to Tlaloc, the god responsible for rain, so he would send rain to the newly planted crops. This is because the tears of children were considered beneficial for summoning rain.

Izcalli
February 4 - 23
Translation: Encouragement for the Land & People

The Aztec lived on the cusp of the cosmic order and its potential collapse into chaos. They had the responsibility to keep their gods happy with their many festivals and rituals, to secure a positive outcome for their people. During the month of Izcalli, their efforts culminated in ritual hunts, sacrifice, and a sacred court dance. The entire month was devoted to fire.

Nemontemi
February 24 - 28
Translation: Empty or Useless Days

As opposed to the neighboring Mayan cultures, who saw these five additional days as a dangerous period, when the worlds between the dead and the living merged, the Aztecs simply saw these last five days as useless. Instead of doing any special rituals to protect themselves from the dead, as

the Maya did, they fasted, abstained from pleasures, such as sexual activity, and generally felt displeased during this time, wishing for the five days to be over soon.	

The Aztec language

The Aztecs called themselves the Mexica, and they spoke Náhuatl. This language belongs to the Uto-Aztecan family tree and was spoken by the Aztec and the Toltec civilization. Since the Aztecs dominated most of the Valley of Mexico during the peak of their civilization, most of the tribes in their kingdom spoke the language.

Later, during the 16th and 17th centuries, Náhuatl also became a literary language, as many important poetic and historical works, including chronicles and administrative documents, were written down in Náhuatl.

Today, the language is still spoken in the regions of central and western Mexico by an estimated 1.5 million people. What's more, many of the words we used in our everyday language have been taken from Náhuatl. Here are some of them.

Hint: These words describe food items, animals, and plants that the Spanish conquistadors encountered for the first time when they discovered the New World. Thus, they absorbed these unfamiliar words into Spanish, as they did not have a better way to describe the exotic things they'd seen.

1. A hot, spicy plant often used to prepare Mexican meals.

C _ _ _ i

2. A nutritious green-skinned fruit, rich in Vitamin B and K.

A _ _ _ _ _ o

3. A wolf-like dog, also called prairie wolf, found mostly in North America.

C_ _ _ _ e

4. A kind of sauce or condiment, made with mashed avocado, chopped onion, tomatoes, and chili peppers. Great with tacos!

G _ _ _ _ _ _ _ e

5. A species of wild cat, found in South America.

O_ _ _ _ t

The Aztec laws and social roles

Aztec daily life was steeped in religious ritual. People also had to 'pay their dues' to their community by setting a prime example, and the nobles were more accountable than commoners on this.

The adults within Aztec society were expected to take care of their children as well as their elders. Only when an Aztec citizen reached the ripe old age of 52 could they live as they wanted to. Elders were often seen drunk in public, and no one raised an eyebrow. By this time, they'd successfully completed their duties, and they no longer owed anything to the society they lived in. In other words, they had retired, and many laws no longer applied to them.

The commoners gave birth to their children at home, in the sweat-baths or *temazcals*. A midwife helped deliver the baby, and she'd stay with the family for a few days, helping the new mother settle into her new role. On the fourth day, the baby was brought into the courtyard to greet the curious neighbours, and bathed in a tub of lake reeds. Three boys would call out the baby's new name - this name was chosen by the midwife, and it was only temporary. The official name was given to them during one of the festivals in May by a priest from the temple.

Only the nobles could choose cool names for their offspring. For example, their king Moctezuma received the great name of 'angry lord.' The day you were born determined your name and destiny. For example, you could be called 'five eagle' or 'two earthquake.' People born on the day of the wind, for example, were considered to be lazy and distracted, drifting around from place to place like the wind.

Each day was governed by a different deity who was responsible for distributing the life energy, or *tonalli,* that the Aztecs believed flowed through every human being. In no particular order, here are some of the days and what it meant if you were born on this day.

Cipactli - the day of the crocodile or dragon.

This day is governed by Tonacatecuhtli, the Lord of Nurturance, according to the Aztec calendar. This day was considered auspicious and signified both honour and advancement to the person born on this day. Energy and work would lead to rewards and recognition later in life.

Cōātl - the day of the serpent.

The day of the Serpent is governed by Chalchihuitlicue. This day was considered as the day of the snaking river that always changes on its own effort without changing. This is symbolic of the fleeting moments, caught in the drift of eternal water. The day of the snake was considered a bad day for acting on self-interests or selfish gains, as the day was reserved for humility.

Ōcēlōtl - the day of the jaguar.

The day of the Jaguar is governed by Tlazolteotl who provided *tonalli* for people born on this day. This was a good day for battle, signifying valour and the right amount of recklessness. This day honoured warriors who sacrificed their lives in the name of others.

If you want to find out the Aztec meaning of your birthday, you can check out this website: https://www.azteccalendar.com/

What happened to your umbilical cord?

Burying their baby's umbilical cord was an important ritual to the Aztecs that tied them to their homes. The umbilical cord of a newborn was buried outside their home. For boys, it was buried under a miniature shield and bow. For girls, it was buried under a grinding stone. This was symbolic to their roots in this home, that would remain there forever, connecting them to their family and ancestry.

Childhood wasn't fun and games for the Aztec kids - at age five, the children of commoners were already hard at work, either doing more physical work if they were boys or helping around the house and cleaning, if they were girls. They soon started school, and following graduation, the boys were enlisted in the army as part of their obligatory service. Their worth as a man was determined not by how many poems they'd written or how beautifully they could sing (all skills they learned at school) but by how many captives they brought back home with them.

The wedding day

People couldn't choose whom they could marry in Aztec society - their relatives and teachers decided on the most suitable life partner for them. Men married by age of 20 while girls were married off at a much younger age - between 10 to 12 years of age.

The wedding day wasn't yours to choose either - it was done by the soothsayers who chose the best possible day for a long and happy marriage. The ceremony took place at the bride's home where guests were served in order of importance (parents and grandparents of the bride and groom were served first, relatives next, and so on). After the wedding feast, the bride was the bathed and dressed at sunset, following which she received something of a lecture from the groom's parents - they reminded her that she was now an adult, and that she must part with her childish age (even though she may have only been 10 years old). The young and indoctrinated bride was then carried over to the groom's house, followed by a procession of the family members, all carrying torches.

Inside the groom's house, the couple sat on a mat, where their robes were tied together, signifying their bond in marriage. (In fact, these ceremonial wedding mats can still be seen in some bridal shops in Mexico and other parts of Latin America to this day). The elders hastily left the house, burning incense in their wake, as they left the couple to enjoy some privacy.

Since they were now adults, they were expected to take care of their elders, allowing them to live with the rest of the family. They also had to carry out their duties at work and care for their children. In fact, raising their children to be good citizens was of utmost importance in Aztec society. All their efforts and finances went toward supporting their children.

Everything the Aztecs did was done only if the priests said so. If the priests believed that a particular day was bad for farming, then no farming was done on that day.

Aside from being farmers, craftsmen, or artisans, the men from the common rank were also warriors, if a time of need arrived. If they were summoned to battle, they had to abandon their homes and go.

Perhaps it's not surprising people finally let loose in their 50s. They no longer had the burden of setting a good public example. The old men no longer needed to go to war, and they could do whatever they liked without any judgment.

The typical diet of an Aztec citizen

While most Aztec diets consisted of maize (or corn), beans and squash, three types of crop that were often grown together across Mesoamerica, your diet varied according to your social rank in society. Everyone enjoyed the occasional fish, rabbit, armadillo, snake, wild turkey or coyote. A commoner or a slave in Tenochtitlán probably enjoyed a better diet than a person of the same rank in Europe.

In addition, people of the Aztec Empire also ate chilies, tomatoes, limes, cashews, sweet potatoes, and peanuts, which was only later introduced in Europe. They also domesticated some animals and insects for food - these included bees, turkeys, and ducks. They also domesticated dogs.

On the gross spectrum, they also ate grasshoppers, iguanas, snakes, and worms, although in minimal amounts. They knew how to make bread and cheese type foods, utilizing a type of algae that grew in the Texcoco lake water.

The Aztec also drank a thick drink called chocolate. The Aztec only drank sugar-free chocolate because they didn't have sugar. They also spiced up their thick chocolate drink by adding peppers, processed corn, and spices. They serve a similar drink in Mexico called atole.

The cocoa bean was so important and treasured that it was used as currency in the markets. The Aztecs believed their god Quetzalcoatl brought them the cocoa bean, after having attained it from the tree of life.

Three delicious Aztec recipes for a healthy Aztec feast!

The cuisine the Aztecs ate would have been different to what we can produce today, but many foods in Mexico have Aztec influences. The Aztecs did not use fat in their cooking but still produced some mouth-watering dishes. Here is our pick of the three best Aztec recipes

Starter - Aztec Tortilla soup

This lovely Aztec Tortilla soup is sure to get your guests' taste buds going. The best part is that you can use stale tortillas for the recipe and they'll taste just as delicious as if they were fresh. This recipe has been 'borrowed' and adapted from Albatz blog. It serves two to four people. You can find the full recipe at http://blogs.ubc.ca/albatz/2012/10/04/eat-like-an-aztec-tortilla-soup-recipe

What you'll need:

- 4 to 8 corn tortillas;
- 1 medium onion;
- 2 garlic cloves;
- 4 or 5 ripe tomatoes;
- 6 cups chicken broth;
- 2 sprigs of epazote;
- salt and pepper for seasoning.

1. Brush the tortillas lightly with corn oil, slice in strips and bake in the oven until crispy.

2. Chop and fry the onion lightly in a little corn oil. Mash the two garlic cloves. Blanch, skin, or grind the tomatoes (alternatively, you can substitute a tin of stewed tomatoes instead) and mash everything together in a saucepan. Add the chicken broth to the stew, along with the epazote. Season and salt to taste.

And if you wanted to give your Aztec soup a fancy finish, you can try adding a couple of avocados, sliced into cubes straight into the soup or on the side, along with some cream cheese and fresh limes. And if you want your tortilla soup to have that Aztec kick, toss in a couple of dried pasilla chilies!

Main course - Aztec chicken

This scrumptious and easy Aztec chicken recipe is sure to hit the spot, even for the hungriest of diners! It serves four people, and you can change some of the ingredients to suit their tastes. The original recipe can be found on the Food Network website that can be accessed via this link http://www.foodnetwork.co.uk/recipes/aztec-chicken.html

What you'll need:

- 6 chicken breast fillets;
- 140g seasoned plain flour;
- 1 egg
- 240ml double cream;
- 240ml olive oil;
- 12 large raw prawns;
- 3 garlic cloves;
- 6 pepperoncini;
- 170g streaky bacon;
- 180ml rum;

- 700ml chicken stock;
- 1 avocado;
- salt and pepper for seasoning.

1. Rub the chicken breasts with some seasoned flour. Crack the eggs into a separate bowl and mix in the cream. Coat the chicken breasts in the egg mixture, so it creates a nice coating. Cook for a few minutes in a saucepan, until the fillets, have turned a lovely golden brown colour and the meat has thoroughly cooked.

2. Add some oil to another saucepan and heat until hot. Drain the excess mixture from the chicken breasts and place them on the frying pan. Now fry the prawns for just a moment, and when they seem halfway done, stir in the crushed garlic, pepperoncini, and chopped bacon.

3. Once you've taken the saucepan off the heat, it's time to add some rum! Pour over your concoction, and light it up with a long match (remember, safety first) and wait for the flames to subside. Add the chicken stock, put the saucepan back on heat and season with salt and pepper to taste. Once it's been frying for a moment, remove ⅓ of the stock and add some avocado. Reduce the heat until the mixture has the consistency of a glaze.

Voila! Your Aztec-worthy main course is ready to be served - place the chicken breasts on a plate, stack the prawns on top and drizzle your delicious glaze over the top.

Dessert - Aztec Hot Chocolate

What could top the delicious taste of a thick, delicious hot chocolate drink! It's like having a hug in a mug. This recipe has been adapted from the Time Traveler Kids website, which can be accessed here:

http://timetravellerkids.co.uk/news/how-to-make-aztec-hot-chocolate/

This recipe could serve anywhere between two to four people, depending on how thirsty they are for some Aztec chocolate!

What you'll need:

- 50g dark chocolate (no sugar allowed);
- a few drops vanilla extract;
- just a pinch of cinnamon and cayenne pepper to spice things up.

1. Break up the chocolate into small squares and place it in a clean saucepan. Pour 300ml of boiling water inside and watch as the chocolate melts. Before it has fully dissolved, add the vanilla extract, cinnamon, and cayenne pepper.

Your chocolate is ready to be served!

Chapter 8 – The Fall of Tenochtitlán

To begin the story of the fall of Tenochtitlán, another story needs to be told. This is the story of one of Mesoamerica's most important gods, Quetzalcóatl ("The Feathered Serpent"). As the name suggests, this god was a serpent with feathers.

Although other Mesoamerican cultures, like the Maya, knew Quetzalcóatl by a different name, most agreed he presided over the rain and winds, and he was also the creator of mankind, and later the creator of the cosmos, along with his brothers Huitzilopochtli and Tezcatlipoca. From 1200 AD onwards, Quetzalcóatl was revered as the patron god of priesthood, learning, science, the arts, and agriculture. Among Quetzalcóatl's inventions were the calendar and the discovery of corn and maize.

Now, we come to a point in the story where, once again, you must make up your own mind as to which side you wish to believe. Most of the material within this chapter comes from the autobiography of Bernal Díaz del Castillo, one of the Spanish conquistadors who wrote his work The True History of the Conquest of New Spain at an old age, many years after the conquest. Although Díaz witnessed every battle for himself and he displayed respect for the locals, he was nonetheless a Spanish soldier who, to some extent, idealised his leader Hernando Cortés. His work is a great adventure story.

In his work, he introduces the idea that, following many successful battles that the Spanish fought against the local tribes before they got to Tenochtitlán, the locals began regarding them as gods. Later, Moctezuma II welcomed the Spaniards in his great city, greeting Cortés as the returning incarnation of Quetzalcóatl. Whether this is true remains debatable. It is certainly one version of the truth - the natives may have had another.

How did the Spaniards get to Tenochtitlán? How did they conquer the vast Aztec empire with only a few hundred soldiers?

The first contact with Europe
Hernando Cortés was not only a brilliant warrior and strategist, he was also an ambitious man and an excellent orator, and this ability saved him on many occasions during the conquest. He landed on the shores

of Mesoamerica in 1519 with only 11 ships, 500 men, 13 horses, and a small number of cannon, ignoring the orders of his former patrón Diego Velázquez de Collar who decided to cancel his mission at the last moment. Upon landing in Yucatan, which was Mayan territory at the time, he established a settlement (now called Veracruz).

A portrait of Hernando Cortés. Source: https://en.wikipedia.org/wiki/Hern%C3%A1n_Cort%C3%A9s

Aside from his troops, Cortés was aided by two important people on his conquest. First, he met Geronimo de Aguilar, a Franciscan priest who'd survived a shipwreck and escaped captivity. Aguilar had learned the local language and became a translator for Cortés. He later met La Malinche or Doña Marina (as she was called by the Spanish), a beautiful indigenous woman who was given to Cortés as a captive. But instead of being his slave, Doña Marina became an important adviser and interpreter (who spoke both Mayan and Náhuatl) during the conquest, and Cortés' mistress, who later gave birth to his son Martín, one of the first 'Mestizos' (people of Native American and European descent).

The road to Tenochtitlán

From the natives Cortés and his crew encountered along the way, he learned of the great wealth of the Aztecs. The Spanish were thirsty for gold, but the Aztecs didn't hold gold in high esteem. Moctezuma II, having found out about their obsession, sent gold to the

Spanish, along with jade jewels and feathers and a message that the king welcomed them, but would only continue to send presents if they stayed away from Tenochtitlán.

While the Spanish were getting closer and closer, Moctezuma II was plagued by a prophecy he'd received from an allied ruler – that enemies would come from the East and this would mark the end of the Aztec empire. According to some accounts, this coincided with the Aztec calendar prophecies that Quetzalcóatl would return in the same year. Whether Moctezuma II really believed that the Spanish were, gods remain open for speculation.

The success of the Spanish conquest was a combination of military force, excellent leadership, and their two trusted interpreters. However, an even more significant role was played by the locals' hostility toward the Aztecs. This is because the Aztecs, a powerful military force, often treated their subjects harshly, asking them to pay steep tributes, and sending their armies to deal with those who refused to pay.

Although at first, they regarded Cortés with suspicion and hostility, the Totonacs and Tlaxcalans eventually joined forces with the Spanish and marched jointly towards Tenochtitlán. In addition, Cortés managed to convince the soldiers sent by his opponents in Europe to join their army on a conquest that the world would never forget. This earned him the loyalty of 400 men, to add to his own army of over 400 men and the support of 2,000 Totonac warriors.

Although many of the locals joined Cortés on his quest, not everything he said went down well. Upon witnessing the acts of human sacrifice, a widespread practice across Mesoamerica, as well as seeing acts of cannibalism and sodomy, Cortés made continuous attempts to educate the locals to stop these practices. In response, the locals were greatly offended, saying they had to do this to appease their gods. They regarded these ideas as insults to their deities. This clash of perception would later play a significant role in the conquest of Tenochtitlán, but more on that later.

The gracious welcome

When Moctezuma II heard about the advances made by the Spanish, he employed several tactics in how to deal with them. As already mentioned, he started by sending them gifts. As the Spanish advanced further and made more allies, they hid thousands of Aztec warriors in one of the cities along the way, but thanks to his informants, Cortés found out about this in time and sacked the city. Moctezuma II sent more messages his way, blaming the locals for conspiring against the Spanish. He finally invited the conquistadors to visit his city. Perhaps this was an act of caution, or perhaps Moctezuma II had surrendered to the fate predicted by the prophecy. Either way, on 8 November 1519 he allowed the Spanish and their indigenous allies to march inside the Aztec capital. Led by Cortés, their entourage entered the city using Iztapalapa, a causeway associated with their god Quetzalcóatl. It was covered in flowers, as Moctezuma II, dressed in fine silks and adorned with feathers and jewels, gave the Spanish a warm and gracious welcome.

He bowed to the Spanish and, according to Bernardino de Sahagún, Florentine Codex, Book 12, Chapter 16, this is what he said in his welcome speech. As you read this, be aware that this again is just one version of the truth.

"Our Lord (..) you have come here to sit on your throne, to sit under its canopy, which I have kept for awhile for you. For the rulers and governors [of past times] have gone: Itzcoatl, Moctezuma I, Axayacatl, Tiçocic, and Ahuitzotl. [Since they are gone], your poor vassal has been in charge for you, to govern the city of Mexico. Will they come back to the place of their absence? If even one came, he might witness the marvel that has taken place in my time, see what I am seeing, as the only descendant of our lords. For I am not just dreaming, not just sleepwalking, not seeing you in my dreams. I am not just dreaming that I have seen you and have looked at you face to face. I have been worried for a long time, looking toward the unknown from which you have come, the mysterious place. For our rulers departed, saying that you would come to your city and sit upon your throne. And now it has been fulfilled; you have returned. Go enjoy your palace, rest your body. Welcome our lords to this land."

And with those words, Moctezuma II led the amazed conquistadors inside his palace where they were made to feel welcome and honoured, treated like gods indeed.

The captive king

The Spanish were welcomed with feasts and tours around the city. They enjoyed all its marvels, and they felt equally amazed and repelled by the city's many practices. Every day they were treated to incredible dance shows, feasts, and human sacrifices. Again, they asked the Aztecs to stop doing what they were doing, that their Christian god disapproved of this, and this created tensions between the Aztecs and the conquistadors (not everyone was as friendly toward them as the king).

Tensions soon built up between the Aztecs and the conquistadors. Although Moctezuma II was urged by his brother Cuitlahuac and nephew Cacamatzin to act against the Spanish, he refuted them. Although plenty of men in his council disagreed with the opinion of their king, Moctezuma II was nonetheless their ruler, and his word was final. It is unclear why he took such a passive stance, but the price he paid was fatal. On 14 November, only a few days after the arrival of the Spanish, Moctezuma II was taken hostage in his palace. Allegedly, it was a peaceful surrender, and the king aided the Spanish conquest from then on. According to some accounts, he became friends with Cortés, sharing long conversations and enjoying board games together.

He allowed the Spanish to remain in his palace and ordered a large tribute of gold and precious gifts to be collected for them. Slowly, the Aztecs started to doubt their own king and turn against him. Tensions escalated at a feast that the Aztecs held in the name of the Spanish.

Massacre at the festival of Tóxcatl

Word reached Cortés that his former patron Velázquez was plotting against him. He sent a force of 19 ships, loaded with more than 800 soldiers, 80 horsemen, 120 crossbowmen and 80 arquebusiers to capture Cortés. The army was led by Pánfilo de Narváez, who was ordered to return Cortés back to Cuba where he would be tried.

When Cortés received the news, he quickly assembled a force of 240 men and left

Tenochtitlán to repel Narváez's forces. He ambushed Narváez's camp late at night, leaving him imprisoned in Veracruz. And what of Narváez's army? Cortés used his orator's talent to charm them with tales of the great Aztec wealth, so they joined his forces and followed him back to the Aztec capital.

Meanwhile, the man whom Cortés had left in command, Pedro de Alvarado, was invited to a feast dedicated to their god Tezcatlipoca. Moctezuma II had attained permission from both Cortés and Alvarado to hold a festival in the honour of this Aztec deity. Alvarado had one condition though - no human sacrifice was allowed. However, the Aztecs had spent a long time preparing to sacrifice a young man who'd impersonated the god Toxcatl for an entire year. Without human sacrifice, their festival was no festival at all!

Alvarado became more suspicious of the Aztecs and ordered the torture of their priests and nobles, who revealed to him the Aztec were planning a revolt. He allowed the festival to commence in the Patio of Dances just outside their great temple. As the dancing grew more euphoric, Alvarado became more agitated. Seeing people feasting on the flesh of other men was the last straw. He went berserk. Alvarado ordered all the gates to be closed and slaughtered everyone on scene - men, women, and children.

While Díaz does not make much of this, the native accounts describe this as a horror they'd never seen before. From their perspective, they were simply celebrating the best of Aztec culture - for them, the festival was filled with beauty and sacredness - and the act of the Spanish was complete sacrilege to their values. A revolt followed, with thousands of Aztecs attacking the conquistadors. They even turned on their own king, who was instructed to give a speech to calm the angry masses.

Once he found out about the events, Cortés hurried back. The roads were shut, and the causeways were drawn or burnt down, so it was difficult for Cortés' forces to get back inside the capital. The Aztecs had stopped supplying the Spanish with food and gifts, disobeying the orders of their king. Just like they'd turned against their king, they now turned against each other, killing those whom they suspected as helping the conquistadors. In one final attempt to restore peace and initiate negotiations, Cortés sent Moctezuma II to give a speech to the maddening crowd. While he spoke, he was hit by a rock and died shortly thereafter. It is said that both Aztecs and the Spanish conquistadors wept over his death. Moctezuma's younger brother Cuitláhuac was elected as the next ruler of the Aztecs.

The Night of Sorrows

"La Noche Triste" or The Night of Sorrows is the name given to the events that followed when the Spanish tried to escape Tenochtitlán on 1 July 1520. Although he risked looking weak in front of the Aztecs and his native allies, Cortés really had no choice but to escape the city. Although they had gathered about 42,000 tons of gold, they could only carry so much with them. The Spanish built platforms from the doors within their compound and lay them across the gaps in causeways, before loading them with gold. This proved to be a disaster, and many of them were captured by the Aztecs. Some drowned in the lake, weighed down by the weight of the gold, while others were captured by the angry Aztecs and dragged to the top of Templo Mayor, where their screams echoed and pierced the ears of Cortés. He lost a third of his army that night, and he is said to have wept under a tree later that night, grieving the loss of so many men.

The Spanish regroup and form alliances

The Spanish found refuge in their allies from Tlacopan. They were headed towards Tlaxcala, chased all the way by the Aztecs. The conquistadors defeated the Aztecs at the Battle of Otumba, but only just. A vital role was played by the shock value of seeing caballeros, or knights on horseback. Five days later, Cortés finally reached Tlaxcala. His losses amounted to 860 Spanish soldiers, more than 1,000 Tlaxcalans, and many Spanish women who had accompanied Narváez. One of Moctezuma II's daughters died as well, leaving behind an infant by Cortés.

Lucky for Cortés, the Tlaxcalans hated the Aztecs so much they became powerful allies of the Spanish. They asked for expensive tributes in return, which Cortés promised. Other allies included the Huexotzinco, Atlixco, Tliliuhqui-Tepecs, Tetzcocans, Chalca, Alcohua and the Tepanecs. Tetzcoco that had been previously allied with Tenochtitlán also joined the Spanish and turned against the Aztecs.

But the Spanish became divided too. Many of the troops wished for nothing more than to return to Veracruz after all they'd been through. But for Cortés, this would mean eventually being captured and convicted as a traitor of the King of Spain. So, he gave another one of his convincing speeches and eventually got his troops to agree to his quest, marching on Tenochtitlán once again. Unknown to them, the Spanish had another powerful ally that killed more people than anyone else - infectious diseases.

The defeat of Tenochtitlán

Smallpox played a crucial role in defeating the Aztecs. In October 1520, an epidemic of smallpox broke out in Tenochtitlán. It was a disease that the Aztecs had not encountered before, probably introduced by one of the slaves from Narváez's ships. The disease raged in the Aztec capital for some 60 days, leading to famine as the local farmers were too sick to tend to their crops. It must be said that the Spanish also suffered losses due to the disease; however, these were less dire than those suffered by the Aztecs. Within a year, almost 40% of the Aztec population had died, including their leader Cuitlahuac, without any effort on the Spanish part.

Although Moctezuma II is often associated with being the last leader of the Aztecs, Cuauhtemoc was their final king. He was elected in February 1521. Weakened by the diseases and still in the process of mourning their dead, the Aztecs stayed within the walls of their once-great city, hoping, wishing, and praying to their gods that the Spanish had gone for good.

But the Spanish were going nowhere. Having regrouped and rounded up their allies, they marched on Tenochtitlán once more. The decisive battle for Tenochtitlán took place between 22 May and 13 August 1521. It was a ninety-three-day siege that Cortés began by ordering an army to guard the entrance to each causeway. By this time, he had a massive army, consisting of his own seasoned men and more than 30,000 native allies. His next step was to cut the aqueducts and prevent a fresh-water supply to the city. Many battles took place during this time, and the Aztecs were victorious in some while defeated in others. Some of the battles were fought along the huge causeways, and the Aztecs used tactics like shooting arrows from canoes to repel the Spanish. Overwhelmed by their force, the Aztec leader Cuauhtemoc decided to escape but was subsequently captured by the Spanish. This led to the Aztec surrender on 13 August 1521.

The future of Tenochtitlán

Following his successful victory, Cortés was recognised as governor and captain-general of New Spain in 1523. The last leader of the Aztecs, Cuauhtemoc, was hanged in 1524 in Chiapas.

However, Cortés was degraded to the position of a civil governor and forced to return to Spain, as the King of Spain feared that he was becoming a tad too powerful. And that was understandable since Cortés had been in charge of an empire containing 500 small city-states with a total population of 6,000,000 indigenous people. He built a new city on the ruins of Tenochtitlán, known today as Mexico City.

Cortés returned to Central America, searching for a route from the Atlantic to the Pacific. He failed in his search, but instead, he found California. He died in 1547, after spending six years on an estate in Seville, allegedly a bitter man.

Conclusion

The ancient Aztecs, along with other Mesoamerican civilizations, were fierce warriors who wanted to attain higher levels of consciousness. For all the wonders of their culture, their tradition of human sacrifice, which they didn't see as a particularly evil practice, horrified the Spanish conquistadors, and gave them a means to justify their conquest. But which party was morally right?

It seems that neither side could perceive the perspective of the other, and neither was interested in doing so. The Spanish condemned the Aztec sacrifices and the Aztecs, in turn, condemned the Spanish for insulting their gods. Greed played a significant role for both parties. Yes, the conquistadors were thirsty for gold, and this cost them many men, but the Aztecs may not have been defeated had it not been for their former allies turning against them, sick and tired of paying so much tribute and taxes to their Aztec overlords.

So, what are we to make of their legacy today, when a new city stands on the rubble of the old world? Who are the people, living in Mexico today? Are they Aztec or Spanish?

It seems the memorial dedicated to three horrific events in the history of Mexico says it best. The Plaza of Three Cultures in Mexico City commemorates the final Battle of Tenochtitlán in 1521, the violent protests of 1968, and the devastating 1985 earthquake.

The Plaza of Three Cultures in Mexico City is also a tribute to the two cultures that clashed (the Spanish and the Aztecs), to eventually give a painful birth to the new culture that inhabits Mexico today - the modern *Mestizo*.

Completed in 1964, the Plaza of Three Cultures is in the exact location where 40,000 Aztecs are said to have died in their final attempt to defend their once-great city. The inscription in the Plaza gives the following account of the conquest of New Spain: "Neither a victory nor a defeat, but the painful moment of birth of the Mexico of today, of a race of *Mestizos*."

Can you help me?

If you enjoyed this book, then I'd really appreciate it if you would post a short review on Amazon. I read all the reviews myself so that I can continue to provide books that people want.

Thanks for your support!

Preview of Maya Civilization

A Captivating Guide to Maya History and Maya Mythology

Introduction

You've probably heard of the Maya and their astounding civilization before. You may recognize the famous Maya calendar that apparently predicted a worldwide apocalypse back in 2012. The media were quick to jump on board this mind-boggling prophecy (which we'll debunk later in this book). Newspapers and websites were filled with stories of doomsday that failed to materialize. Lucky for us, we did wake up on December 22, 2012, when the Maya calendar apparently ended.

But what you may not know is how much the Maya legacy is impacting your life today. Do you love to treat yourself to a frothy hot chocolate before bed, or indulge in an after-dinner chocolate treat? Do you love adding a side of fries to your meal? What about tomatoes for your favorite Italian dishes? If you do, you may not be aware that you have the Maya and the Spanish conquistadors to thank, for they introduced these goods to Europe and other continents.

But Maya are far more than just their food. In this captivating guide, you'll discover why Maya have gained such worldwide admiration over the many other civilizations that existed in Mesoamerica at the time. You'll learn how the Maya civilization developed, the major turning points in their 3,000-year-long history, the mysteries surrounding their demise, and some of the unique places where Maya exist to this day.

Oh yes. If you think the Maya are gone, think again. As opposed to popular belief, the Maya are neither extinct, nor quiet. They are six-million strong, according to some sources, most of them living in Guatemala. What's more, in 1994 one of the surviving Maya tribes, the Zapatistas, launched a rebellion in southeast Mexico against global trade and capitalism.

In the first part of this book, we'll first examine the origins of the Maya civilization and the Mesoamerican cultures that may have influenced them. We'll discuss why Maya (out of all the different tribes that existed in the region at the time) have captured the imagination of the West so much. We'll look at how they lived, ate, slept, whom they worshipped, and how they used herbal medicines and hallucinogenic plants to treat the sick.

We'll look at their trading routes and rivalries with another famous Mesoamerican tribe—the Aztecs. We'll look into the decline of the Maya civilization and how their rivalries with the Aztecs aided the victory of the Spanish conquistadors in the 16th century, led by the famous Spaniard Hernán Cortés. We won't forget to mention the heroic efforts of the Maya to fend off the Spaniards, and why they were able to succeed at this task for much longer than the Aztecs. We'll even track down the Maya living today, a population that is still six-million strong and adhere to many of the traditions that their ancestors once held. In among the battle tales and gore of human sacrifice, we'll look at some delicious cocoa recipes, Maya-style, that you can make at home.

After we've learnt all about the Maya origins, their cuisine, and their most notable events to present day, we'll delve into the aspect that's often the reason why so many people have been fascinated by the Maya civilization throughout the ages. We will look at their mythology, cosmology, and the solar calendar that resulted in the infamous doomsday scare back in 2012.

So buckle up and get ready to be transported to the warm and wet plains of the Maya civilization—it will be a journey you'll never forget.

Maya Timeline

The Archaic Period:

- 7000 to 2000 BC

The Preclassic Period:

- Early Preclassic – 2000 to 1000 BC
- Middle Preclassic – 1000 to 300 BC
- Late Preclassic – 300 BC to AD 250

The Classic Period:

- Early Classic – AD 250 to 600

- Late Classic – AD 600 to 900
- Terminal Classic – AD 900 to 1000

The Postclassic Period:

- Early Postclassic – AD 1000 to 1250
- Late Postclassic – AD 1250 to 1521
- The Spanish Invasion – AD 1521

Glossary of Important Maya Terms

- Cacao – the seeds that the Maya used in order to create their delicious cacao drink, also known as "bitter water."

- Cenote – a type of sink-hole that the Maya used to get fresh supplies of water (and to perform ritual sacrifice).

- Conquistadors – the Spanish military leaders who led the conquest of America in the 16th century, including Hernándo Cortés.

- The Dresden Codex – located in a museum in Germany, the Dresden Codex is one of the oldest surviving books from the Americas. It contains 78 pages with important information on rituals, calculations, and the planetary movements of Venus.

- Haab – one of the several Maya calendars (this one measured time in 365-day cycles).
- Hero Twins – the central characters in the Maya creation story and the ancestors of future Maya rulers.
- Huipil – traditional dress for Maya women.
- Maize – the staple food of Maya civilization, an ancient form of corn (the Maize god was one of the most important deities for Maya).
- Mesoamerica – this is what we call the region of the Americas before the arrival of the Spanish fleets and its colonisation in the 15th and 16th centuries.
- Popol Vuh – the story of creation of the world that was passed down from generation to generation (it was recorded by the Quiche Maya who lived

in the region of modern day Guatemala).

- Shamanism – an important spiritual practice throughout Mesoamerica (during shamanic trance a shaman would be able to practice divination and healing).
- Stelae – an upright stone slab or column, often used as a gravestone. These structures usually contained commemorative inscriptions.
- Yucatan Peninsula – a region in the southeast of Mexico, where some of the Maya civilization developed, especially in the Postclassic period.

Part 1 – History

Chapter 1: The Origins of the Mesoamerican Civilizations

Maya have captivated the imagination of the West ever since their culture was "discovered" in the 1840s by the American writer and explorer John Lloyd Stephens and the English artist and architect Frederick Catherwood. The latter is best known for his intricate and detailed images of the Maya ruins that he and Stephens later published in their book *Incidents of Travel in Central America*.

But just because the West didn't discover the Maya until the mid-nineteenth century doesn't mean that they lived in obscurity the rest of the time. In fact, their history is rich with fantastical tales and splendour and a diet that people living in other regions at the time could only dream about. The origins of the Maya civilization can be traced all the way back to 7,000 BC.

The Archaic period: 7000 – 2000 BC
People were once hunter-gatherers, living a largely nomadic lifestyle, according to the whims of nature and the sharp-toothed animals all around them. They had to keep moving in order to stay safe and keep up their food supplies. But in 7000 BC a new shift began—the hunter-gatherers who lived in Mesoamerica discovered something that would change their region forever. They began planting crops.

It's not entirely clear why this shift occurred when it did. The changing weather patterns may have had something to do with it—the climate gradually became wetter and warmer, so many of the larger animals that the Mesoamericans relied on for food became extinct. As a result, they had to eat more plants and grains, so eventually they started growing some for themselves. They used many techniques to make their lands more fertile. For example, they discovered that burning trees helped put nitrates into the soil to make it more fertile. (Don't try this at home.)

As a result, these ancient people started having a much more varied diet. We know this thanks to the discoveries by the archaeologists working in the Tehuacan Valley of Mexico, a site that contains the best evidence for human activity in the Archaic time period in Mesoamerica. The locals were able to plant and eat things that we often take for granted today, such as peppers, squash, and avocado. Not to mention early forms of corn, the grain that would become the staple food in Mesoamerica.

Since they were able to grow the food that they needed in order to survive, these ancient people no longer needed to move around as much. They began settling down into small villages, leading to the first known settlements in Mesoamerica. The first evidence of individual burial spots directly under people's homes dates back to 2600 BC. These early settlements included temples and sacred spots for worship, suggesting an early form of a civilization. Temples, worship, and sacrifice remained a prominent theme throughout the Maya history, and we'll cover more of it later.

But the Maya did not evolve in a vacuum. There were many cultures and tribes that existed around them, and each had some influence on their culture, customs, and civilization. We'll examine these, one at a time, as we travel through time to really appreciate the interplay between those cultures and the Maya. Before we go onto learning about how these early settlements evolved into the Maya civilization, let's look at one of the most important tribes that existed in Mesoamerica at the time—the Olmecs.

The Olmecs: 1,200 – 300 BC

No one really knows where the Olmecs came from or where they disappeared to. But their legacy on the Mesoamerican tribes, including the Maya, is huge.

The Olmecs inhabited the area along the Gulf of Mexico, and their impressive stone cities gave way to myths about giants who may have lived in this area at the time. The Olmec craftsmanship was highly sophisticated—there are some impressive sculptures that survive to this day as evidence of their superb skills.

Sometimes ancient history is a bit of guesswork, leaving you to fill in the gaps left out by missing evidence. It's interesting that there's a total lack of battle scenes in the Olmec art—something that most other cultures are quick to display in their monuments and sculptures. The fact that they depict no battle scenes could mean one of two things. Either they did not engage in any war conflict, or they simply didn't feel like showing off about it. You decide.

Until recently, the Olmecs were regarded as the "mother culture" of all the great Mesoamerican civilizations to come, including the Maya and the Aztecs. But more recent sources argue that the Maya actually had a counter-influence on the Olmecs.

When it comes to the Olmec mythology, displayed in their surviving temples and sculptures, there are definite traces of shamanic practice. Many of their sculptures depict a were-jaguar, a core element of shamanism, symbolizing shamanic trance. The Maya saw the jaguar as a transformational animal, who feels at home at night-time, a symbol for the Underworld. The symbolism of shamanistic practice is present in all later Mesoamerican cultures, including the Maya.

The Olmecs may have had an important motif of a twin deity, that may have influenced the mythology of the Maya Hero Twins. The Hero Twins is a way to express the duality that the Maya saw around them—the complementary duality between day and night, life and death, the masculine and the feminine. The Olmec flaming eyebrows, the first corn, and cross bands are all symbols that would later appear in the Maya art, connected to astrology. Ancestor worship was also prevalent in the Olmec tradition, as it was later in the Maya and most Mesoamerican cultures at the time.

Challenge your perceptions—Dwarfism
When studying ancient history and learning about cultures, it's always interesting to find out what light it can shed on the culture that we inhabit today. Sometimes the things that we perceive as true are to do with our cultural upbringing. For example, nowadays we define people who are born with smaller organisms and don't grow much taller than 147cm as having the medical condition of Dwarfism or "short stature." We tend to see this as an abnormality, assuming that people born with

this condition would face certain limitations in life.

Well, the Olmec also saw Dwarfism as an abnormality, only not a limiting one. In fact, it was quite the opposite. As the director of the Maya Exploration Center, Dr. Edwin Barnhart explains in his audio-lecture series *Maya To Aztec: Ancient Mesoamerica Revealed* that if you were born with a very small organism in the Olmec or the later Maya culture, you'd be seen as a magical being, touched by the gods. You'd be enjoying all kinds of luxuries, often appearing in the king's court. This may be something to do with their belief that the sky was held up by four dwarves, and so they gave them special treatment.

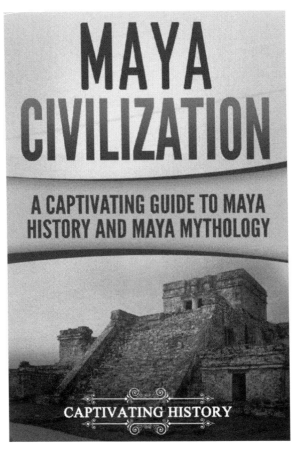

Check out this book!

Make sure to check out more books
by Captivating History

Free Bonus from Captivating History (Available for a Limited time)

Hi History Lovers!

Now you have a chance to join our exclusive history list so you can get your first history ebook for free as well as discounts and a potential to get more history books for free! Simply visit the link below to join.

Captivatinghistory.com/ebook

Also, make sure to follow us on:

Twitter: @Captivhistory

Facebook: Captivating History:
@captivatinghistory

Bibliography

Introduction

Barnhart, E. (2015). *Maya to Aztec: Ancient Mesoamerica Revealed.* Chapter 33: Arrival and Rise of the Mexica. The Great Courses. [Audiobook].

Aztec Group. *The Aztec Civilization.* [online] Available at http://aztecgroup.blogspot.co.uk/p/aztec-environment.html [Accessed 8 Sept 2017].

Chapters 1 & 2

Barnhart, E. (2015). *Maya to Aztec: Ancient Mesoamerica Revealed.* Chapter 33: Arrival and Rise of the Mexica. The Great Courses. [Audiobook].

Aztec History (2006). *Aztec Flower War.* [online] Available at: http://www.aztec-history.com/aztec-flower-war.html [Accessed 8 Sept 2017].

Maestri, Nicoletta (2017). *Aztec Origins and the Founding of Tenochtitlan.* [online] Available at https://www.thoughtco.com/aztec-origins-the-founding-of-tenochtitlan-170038 [Accessed 8 Sept 2017].

Bitto, Robert (2016). *Journey to Aztlán, the Mythical Homeland of the Aztecs.* [online] Available at http://mexicounexplained.com/journey-aztlan-mythical-homeland-aztecs/ [Accessed 9 Sept 2017].

Jarus, Owen (2017). Tenochtitlán: History of Aztec Capital. [online] Available at https://www.livescience.com/34660-tenochtitlan.html [Accessed 7 Sept 2017].

Jorge, M et al. (2011). *Mathematical accuracy of Aztec land surveys assessed from records in the Codex Vergara*. PNAS: University of Michigan.

Chapter 3

Cortes, Hernando. *Letters of Cortés: five letters of relation to the Emperor Charles V.* [online] Available at: https://archive.org/stream/lettersofcorts01cortuoft/lettersofcorts01cortuoft_djvu.txt [Accessed 3 Sept 2017]

Barnhart, E. (2015). *Maya to Aztec: Ancient Mesoamerica Revealed.* Chapter 29: The Toltecs: Role Models or Myth? The Great Courses. [Audiobook].

Maestri, Nicoletta (2017). *Aztec Triple Alliance - Foundations of the Aztec Empire.* [online] Available at: https://www.thoughtco.com/aztec-triple-alliance-170036 [Accessed Sept 5 2017]

Chapter 4

Wikipedia. *Acamapichtli.* [online] Available at:
https://en.wikipedia.org/wiki/Acamapichtli
[Accessed Sept 5 2017]

Wikipedia. *Huitzilihuitl.* [online] Available at:
https://en.wikipedia.org/wiki/Huitzilihuitl
[Accessed Sept 5 2017]

Ancient History Encyclopedia. *Aztec
Civilization Timeline.* [online] Available at:
http://www.ancient.eu/timeline/Aztec_Civilizat
ion/ [Accessed Sept 6 2017]

Soustelle, Jacques et al. *Pre-Columbian
civilizations.* [online] Available at:
https://www.britannica.com/topic/pre-
Columbian-civilizations#ref583519 [Accessed
Sept 7 2017]

Tenochtitlán Facts. *Montezuma I.* [online]
Available at:
http://www.tenochtitlanfacts.com/Montezuma
-I.html [Accessed Sept 4 2017]

Tenochtitlán Facts. *Axayacatl.* [online]
Available at:

http://www.tenochtitlanfacts.com/Axayacatl.html [Accessed Sept 4 2017]

Hassig, Ross (1988). Aztec Warfare: Imperial Expansion and Political Control. Norman: University of Oklahoma Press. p. 10.

Chapters 5 & 6

Barnhart, E. (2015). *Maya to Aztec: Ancient Mesoamerica Revealed.* Chapter 34: The Aztec Capital of Tenochtitlán. The Great Courses. [Audiobook].

Barnhart, E. (2015). *Maya to Aztec: Ancient Mesoamerica Revealed.* Chapter 35: Life in the Aztec World. The Great Courses. [Audiobook].

Cartwright, Mark (2016). *Templo Mayor.* [online] Available at: http://www.ancient.eu/Templo_Mayor/ [Accessed Sept 5 2017]

Klimczak, Natalia (2016). *Montezuma Zoo: A Legendary Treasure of the Aztec Empire* [online] Available at: http://www.ancient-origins.net/ancient-places-americas/montezuma-zoo-legendary-treasure-aztec-empire-005090 [Accessed Sept 6, 2017]

Mexicolore (2010). *Aztec Pleasure Gardens.* [online] Available at: http://www.mexicolore.co.uk/aztecs/aztefacts/aztec-pleasure-gardens [Accessed Sept 7 2017]

Chapter 7

Wikipedia. Aztec Calendar. [online] Available at: https://en.wikipedia.org/wiki/Aztec_calendar [Accessed Sept 8 2017]

History on the Net. *Aztec Religious Ceremonies and Rituals.* [online] Available at: http://www.historyonthenet.com/aztec-religious-ceremonies-and-rituals/ [Accessed Sept 9 2017]

Graulich, Michael. *Aztec Festivals of the Rain Gods.* [online] Available at:http://www.iai.spk-berlin.de/fileadmin/dokumentenbibliothek/Indi

ana/Indiana_12/IND_12_Graulich.pdf
[Accessed Sept 9 2017]

Haunty. *Ancient Aztec Festivals, Celebrations and Holidays.* [online] Available at:
https://owlcation.com/humanities/Ancient-Aztec-Festivals-Celebrations-and-Holidays
[Accessed Sept 7 2017]

University of California. *Realms of the Sacred in Daily Life: Early Written Records of Mesoamerica* [online] Available at:
https://www.lib.uci.edu/sites/all/exhibits/meso/aztec3.html [Accessed Sept 6, 2017]

Roy, Christian. *Traditional Festivals: A Multicultural Encyclopedia, Volume 1.* 2005. California: ABC Clio. p. 211. [online] Available at:
https://books.google.co.uk/books?id=IKqOUfqt4cIC&dq=Izcalli+aztec+rituals&source=gbs_navlinks_s [Accessed Sept 3 2017]

Chapter 8

History. *Aztecs.* [online] Available at:
www.history.com/topics/aztecs [Accessed
Sept 2 2017]

Barnhart, E. (2015). *Maya to Aztec: Ancient
Mesoamerica Revealed.* Chapter 29: The
Toltecs: Role Models or Myth? [Audiobook].

Cartwright, Michael. *Quetzalcoatl.* [online]
Available at:
http://www.ancient.eu/Quetzalcoatl/
[Accessed Sept 5 2017]

The Editors of Encyclopædia Britannica. *Bernal
Díaz del Castillo.* [online] Available at:
https://www.britannica.com/biography/Bernal
-Diaz-del-Castillo [Accessed Sept 7 2017]

American Historical Association. *Mexica
Accounts of Moctezuma Meeting Cortes.*
[online] Available at:
https://www.historians.org/teaching-and-
learning/teaching-resources-for-
historians/teaching-and-learning-in-the-
digital-age/the-history-of-the-americas/the-
conquest-of-mexico/florentine-codex/mexica-

accounts-of-moctezuma-meeting-cortes
[Accessed 6 Sept 2017]

Conclusion

Barnhart, E. (2015). *Maya to Aztec: Ancient Mesoamerica Revealed.* Chapter 42: The Siege of Tenochtitlan [Audiobook].

ABOUT CAPTIVATING HISTORY

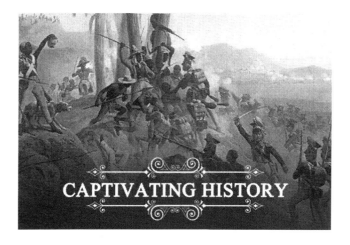

A lot of history books just contain dry facts that will eventually bore the reader. That's why Captivating History was created. Now you can enjoy history books that will mesmerize you. But be careful though, hours can fly by, and before you know it; you're up reading way past bedtime.

Get your first history book for free here:
http://www.captivatinghistory.com/ebook

Make sure to follow us on Twitter:

@CaptivHistory

and Facebook:

www.facebook.com/captivatinghistory so you

can get all of our updates!

Made in the USA
Columbia, SC
13 January 2019